VICTORIAN
LONDON

VICTORIAN LONDON

LEE JACKSON
& ERIC NATHAN

NEW HOLLAND

First published in 2004 by New Holland Publishers (UK) Ltd
London • Cape Town • Sydney • Auckland

www.newhollandpublishers.com

Garfield House, 86–88 Edgware Road, London W2 2EA,
United Kingdom

80 McKenzie Street, Cape Town 8001, South Africa

14 Aquatic Drive, Frenchs Forest, NSW 2086, Australia

218 Lake Road, Northcote, Auckland, New Zealand

10 9 8 7 6 5 4 3 2 1

ISBN 1 84330 734 0

Publishing Manager: Jo Hemmings
Senior Editor: Kate Michell
Assistant Editor: Rose Hudson
Cover Design and Design: Alan Marshall
Production: Joan Woodroffe

Reproduction by Modern Age Repro Co. Ltd, Hong Kong
Printed and bound in Singapore by Kyodo Printing Co. (Singapore)
Pte Ltd

Photographs appearing on the cover and prelim pages are as follows:
Front cover: The Albert Memorial in Kensington Gardens.
Spine: The Victoria Memorial, The Mall.
Front flap: Tower Bridge, built 1896.
Back cover (left): Turkish Baths, Bishopsgate; (centre): The Ducrow
Monument, Kensal Green Cemetery; (right): Crossness Pumping
Station interior, east London.
Back flap: Simpson's-in-the-Strand restaurant.
Title page: Decorative detail from a Victorian lamppost.
Page 2: Crossness Pumping Station interior, east London.
Page 3: A traditional Victorian shop front.
Opposite page: Hotel Russell, Russell Square.
Page 6 (left): A Victorian parlour as seen in the Geffrye Museum,
Hackney; (right): The Victoria Memorial, The Mall.
Page 7 (left): The Ducrow Monument, Kensal Green Cemetery;
(right): The Princess Louise interior, Holborn.

AUTHOR'S ACKNOWLEDGEMENTS
I would like to thank the following:
    Joanne for everything, but especially the commas; Mum and
Dad for buying me too many books; the good people at New
Holland, for taking an interest in Victorian London; the workers in
London's museums and libraries, who continue to make The Great
Metropolis a magical place for Victorian enthusiasts; the shops and
businesses who consented to have their likeness taken for the pur-
pose of this book; and, finally, the friendly scholars of the Victoria
discussion list for answering many of my stupid questions.
                                    Lee Jackson, December 2003

CONTENTS

INTRODUCTION

'So you were never in London before?' said Mr Wemmick to me.

'No,' said I.

'I was new here once,' said Mr Wemmick. 'Rum to think of now!'

'You are well acquainted with it now?'

'Why, yes,' said Mr Wemmick. 'I know the moves of it.'

CHARLES DICKENS, *GREAT EXPECTATIONS*, 1861

What was life like in Victorian London?

Above all, contemporary commentators were struck by the sheer size of the capital. This was no mere city, but rather 'The Great Metropolis', a 'nation in itself', a place where one might observe every conceivable form of human activity and endeavour. Indeed, writers often chose to describe it as a 'beehive', an image popular with the Victorians, evoking not only frenetic activity, but industry and productivity. London was vast, dynamic, restless – the greatest city in the world. Certainly it was the largest; by the 1890s its population was fifty per cent greater than that of New York or Paris, its nearest rivals.

Great riches and dire poverty

Admittedly, some despaired when they considered London's increasing size, lamenting the engulfment of the surrounding countryside by suburban housing. However, there was also a sense of exhilaration, a growing pride in the creation of an Imperial capital that served as the beating heart of a great Empire.

The face of London changed dramatically during Queen Victoria's reign (1837–1901) in response to increasing demands placed upon the city's infrastructure. New roads were cut through slums; a vast network of sewers was constructed; ten new bridges were built over the Thames, and three tunnels beneath it; railway stations, grand hotels, viaducts, embankments, the marvel of the underground railway – the list is endless. It is hardly surprising that, by the end of the nineteenth century, it was commonly believed that the wonders of The Great Metropolis rivalled, or even outshone, the glories of ancient Rome.

Nevertheless, everyone knew full well what lurked beneath the grandeur – poverty. Here, too, was a city where mudlarks still sifted the muddy banks of the Thames, scavenging the filth for discarded pieces of coal or iron. Poor men and women earned precarious livings, hawking goods on the street, selling anything from bird seed to picture postcards, to make a few pence. Others toiled in sweatshops or 'manufactories', working long hours under difficult and debilitating conditions, often for a pittance. Prostitution was commonplace and highly visible, whether one looked for it in the darkest East End or in the bright lights of the Haymarket and Leicester Square. And, much like today, 'strangers and country folk' were frequently advised of the trickery of thieves and beggars.

Not for nothing, then, was the city also known as 'the modern Babylon', a phrase suggesting not

Above: *The statue of Eros was erected in Piccadilly Circus in 1893 as a representation of 'The Angel of Christian Charity'.*
Opposite: *Initiated by Prince Albert, and named in his memory, the Royal Albert Hall opened in 1871 as a public concert hall.*

only immense wealth and luxury, but a strong undercurrent of dissipation and sin.

So, what *was* life like in Victorian London?

For some, London seemed blessed by immense prosperity, full of breathtaking examples of 'progress'; for others, it resembled a sea of misery and squalor. And, doubtless, in between these two extremes lay the experience of millions of Londoners.

Living History

Of course, no single book can encompass such diversity. My intention is merely to provide some 'hints' (to borrow a word from Victorian guidebooks) in relation to certain topics, so that, like Charles Dickens's Mr Wemmick, my readers may come to 'know the moves' of Victorian London. In particular, I hope this book will prove useful for anyone who wishes to actively explore the many parts of the nineteenth-century city that survive to this day.

Indeed, if you happen to reside in London, or merely pay a visit, you do not have to dig deep for its Victorian roots. From the humblest terraced house to the grandest West End theatre, much of the bricks and mortar of the Victorian world is still in use. Furthermore, if you spend time walking around the city, you may notice that, like their nineteenth-century forebears, modern Londoners travel either by 'underground railway', 'omnibus' or 'hackney cab'. They, too, drink in 'public houses' and visit 'shopping arcades'. On occasion, they even complain about the weather, although perhaps with less justification.

Victorian London is still here; and we are living in it.

LEISURE TIME

TOURISM

SIGHT-SEEING in the opinion of many experienced travellers, is best avoided altogether… One piece of advice to the intending sight-seer is at all events sound. Never go to see anything by yourself. If the show be a good one, you will enjoy yourself all the more in company; and the solitary contemplation of anything that is dull and tedious is one of the most depressing experiences of human life.

CHARLES DICKENS JR, *DICKENS'S DICTIONARY OF LONDON*, 1879

Above: Thomas Cook's tour company arranged for 165,000 visitors to travel to London for the Great Exhibition of 1851.

Opposite: The sumptuous interior of the Garrick Theatre, Charing Cross Road, which opened in 1889.

Below: St Paul's Cathedral has always been a popular attraction. In the nineteenth century, it cost 2d. to enter the cathedral, 6d. to visit the galleries and 1s. to enter the crypt.

Charles Culliford Dickens (1837–96), son of the great novelist, Charles Dickens, lived somewhat in the shadow of his famous father. He did, however, write one rather interesting book himself – *Dickens's Dictionary of London*, a guide to the metropolis that was first published in 1879. Subtitled 'An Unconventional Handbook', it was arranged alphabetically, and contained everything a Victorian sightseer might wish to know about the capital, including bus timetables, lists of theatres and famous landmarks and advice on finding a policeman. It also included various amusing asides, not least the deliberate irony, quoted above, of advising readers against 'sight-seeing'.

Yet, for all its merits, *Dickens's Dictionary of London* was hardly 'unconventional'. It was, in fact, one of numerous London guidebooks available to the Victorians. Such books generally included a pocket street atlas and brief descriptions of places and sights. For, as today, the teeming streets of Victorian London were often crowded, not only with local residents, but also with tourists.

Holidaymakers and Daytrippers

Mass tourism was a Victorian invention. True, in the eighteenth century, individual members of the aristocracy had indulged themselves in 'Grand Tours' of Europe, especially among the classical ruins of Italy and Greece, but the nineteenth century was different. The spread of the railways in the 1830s and 1840s meant it was suddenly possible to transport large numbers of people considerable distances for the purposes of leisure and amusement.

Pioneers, such as Thomas Cook, whose travel firm survives to this day, began to organize 'package tours' to popular regional destinations. Seaside resorts, in particular, prospered enormously as a result. London

11

in its turn, as the great railway termini opened – London Bridge, Euston and Paddington in the 1830s, Fenchurch Street and Waterloo in the 1840s – began to receive an ever-increasing number of tourists, armed with their guidebooks and anxious to see the places and sights of the capital.

The Sights

What did they come to see? In a sense, one can get a good idea of the Victorian visitor's experience of London by following the modern tourist trail. This is simply a testament to the endurance of London's historic buildings and monuments. The prime examples, of course, are the great churches of Westminster Abbey and St Paul's Cathedral. St Paul's has charged visitors for admission since its opening, in 1709. One might also list the Tower of London, the Monument to the Great Fire of London, which was completed in 1677 – though the railings are a Victorian addition, following a spate of suicide jumps in the 1830s and 1840s – the Royal Naval College at Greenwich, which was established in 1694 and planned by Sir Christopher Wren, and numerous churches. The Victorians loved to visit these magnificent buildings, just as we do today.

However, there was one quintessentially Victorian 'visitor attraction' that drew more visitors to London than anything that came before it.

THE GREAT EXHIBITION

I dare say you have seen pictures of the Crystal Palace in Hyde Park—the building which was erected for the Great Exhibition of 1851. It was designed by Mr. Paxton, who rose from being a gardener's boy to be 'Sir Joseph Paxton, M.P.' Built almost entirely of iron and glass, it had a beautiful fairy-like appearance; and though it was nearly twice the breadth and fully four times the length of St Paul's Cathedral, covering twenty acres of ground, it had a gay, lightsome look, which was a pleasing novelty amongst our public buildings. It was opened by the Queen on May 1st, 1851, and continued open till the 11th of October. During those one hundred and forty-four days of exhibition it was visited by more than six millions *of persons.*

'UNCLE JONATHAN', *WALKS IN AND AROUND LONDON*, 1895

It is difficult to overestimate the impact the Great Exhibition made upon the British public. The best index of its popularity is that six million tickets were sold in six months, at a time when Britain's total population was only about twenty million. In the provinces, whole towns and villages seemed to empty overnight when the local 'excursion club' made the train journey to the capital. The streets of London, meanwhile, thronged with visitors.

The Crystal Palace

Upon arriving in Hyde Park, the first thing the crowds saw was the marvellous spectacle of the iron-and-glass exhibition building: the 'Crystal Palace'. It was over 1,800 feet long and 450 feet wide; cruciform in shape, with long naves and a north and south transept; and a 27-foot high 'crystal fountain' at the central intersection. Its domed roof was high enough to accommodate within its precincts the park's large trees.

Above: The Egyptian Court was a new introduction to the Crystal Palace when it relocated to Sydenham, south London, and was one of several galleries with a historical theme.

Opposite: Two hundred and forty-five plans for the Great Exhibition building were rejected before Joseph Paxton's 'Crystal Palace', based on a greenhouse design, was chosen.

As for the actual contents of the exhibition, the project's full title was 'The Great Exhibition of the Works of Industry of all Nations', but principally it was meant to provide a showcase for British manufacturing. Artworks, machinery and curiosities from around the globe competed for space in the galleries, which spread over two floors. The American traveller David Bartlett described his visit, which took in 'models of bridges-telescopes-lighthouses and docks... a fine collection of cottons, wools, seeds, native arms, and artillery from the British East Indies... English hardware agricultural implements, and woven fabrics... a splendid collection of carriages... cotton-mills in full operation, printing presses striking off impressions of newspapers and all kinds of curious machines requiring steam motive power... the Koh-i-noor diamond... embroidery, silks, musical instruments... libraries, bronzes, tapestry, gold and silversmith's work, laces, blondes, artificial flowers and statuary... toys, boots and shoes... [the] electric tele-graph, embroideries, carpet-work... brocades, silks, muslins and furs...locomotives... bronze castings, raw silks and statuary... porcelain vases, ornamental cabinet-work, Florentine mosaics...'. Doubtless, like many others, he left Hyde Park quite exhausted.

When the exhibition closed in October 1851, there were immediate calls for it to reopen. Unfortunately, the Hyde Park site had always been intended to be temporary, as there were fears the crowds would permanently lower the tone of the area. This was a particular concern to fashionable London, since it was customary during the summer months for the aristocracy to take leisurely drives along the park's wide avenues, showing off their latest carriages.

Above: *Stone sphinxes, modelled on the Great Sphinx at Tanis, Egypt, once guarded the steps up to the Crystal Palace in its new site in Sydenham in south-east London.*

Relocation by Popular Demand

Luckily, because of the exhibition's unprecedented popularity, and the ease with which its pre-fabricated structure could be reassembled, wholesale relocation was considered feasible. Work soon began on rebuilding the 'Palace', substantially enlarged, at Sydenham in south-east London. This second version was officially opened by the Queen and Prince Albert in June 1854, and was even more magnificent than its predecessor. It contained numerous new 'Courts' in Assyrian, Egyptian, Greek, Roman and medieval styles, to name but a few – portions of Spain's Alhambra Palace had even been replicated. There were also extensive landscaped grounds.

The south-east London location was equally successful, and also hosted temporary exhibitions. The main building went on to provide the venue for events as diverse as a triennial Handel Festival, temperance meetings and dog shows. The grounds were also regularly used for sporting competitions, such as archery, athletics and football.

Tragically, the Crystal Palace was spectacularly destroyed by fire in 1936. Today, it is a rather eerie location, well off the tourist map, with steps that now lead nowhere and the site of the former palace guarded by crumbling stone sphinxes and decapitated statues. Bizarrely, the only things that have survived fully intact at Sydenham are twenty-nine 'life-size' models of dinosaurs, built in the grounds for educational purposes. They were created at a time when debate over evolutionary theory rendered the giant lizards fascinating to the general public. Made from brick, reinforced with iron and finished with stucco, the creatures were refurbished in 2003.

Deserving Popularity

In retrospect, it is hardly surprising that tourists flocked to the Crystal Palace in 1851. Nothing quite like it had been seen before. True, there were museums in London, but there had never been anything quite so modern, containing the latest technical advances, nor any spectacle quite so dazzling. As the crowds surged through Hyde Park, railwaymen, omnibus owners, cabbies, hoteliers and sellers of maps and guidebooks, all rubbed their hands with glee – tourists meant profits. Schweppes, the soft drinks manufacturer had the contract for refreshments at the exhibition, and sold over a million bottles of soda water, lemonade and ginger beer. 'Gelatine cards' (picture postcards) showing representations of the Crystal Palace were among the most popular items sold by street hawkers.

Here was an attraction that proved popular with all classes of society, even if some doubts were initially expressed concerning the admittance of 'shilling people'. Built for the noble purpose of promoting British industry and achievement, the exhibition fostered patriotism, social harmony and educated the masses – all under one glass roof. It even boosted the status of the monarchy, as Prince Albert, never before a favourite with the British people, was widely known to be its most ardent and vocal proponent.

LESSER EXHIBITIONS

SOUTH LONDON WORKING CLASSES INDUSTRIAL EXHIBITION… The objects [of the exhibition] are stated to be the bringing to light the ingenious contrivances of working men; to show that hours well improved (instead of being spent in idleness, or, worse still, the public-house) may produce results astonishing to the working men themselves… The number of exhibitors was stated to be 125, and articles exhibited 500, and these are classified under seven heads. 1. Useful. 2. Ingenious. 3. Ornamental. 4. Scientific. 5 and 6 Artistic and Literary. 7. Curious and Amusing. A catalogue is sold for one penny; the admission is two pence each person.

JOURNAL OF THE SOCIETY OF ARTS, 1864

It was natural that there would be attempts to repeat the Great Exhibition's success, beginning with the 1862 International Exhibition in Kensington. Although somewhat overshadowed by the death of Prince Albert in 1861, it still attracted hordes of visitors, and a series of smaller annual International Exhibitions, in Kensington again, began in 1871.

In the suburbs, meanwhile, there were small 'working men's exhibitions' in an attempt to educate the poor. Then, in 1886, came the Colonial and Indian Exhibition, a 'practical demonstration of the wealth and industrial development of the outlying portions of the British Empire'. If these later projects never quite recaptured the novelty and excitement of the original Great Exhibition, they did not lack for visitors. The 'American Exhibition' at Earl's Court,

Above: *A forerunner to the London Eye, the Great Wheel at Earl's Court (1895–1907) was based on the Great Wheel invented by G. W. G. Ferris for the 'World's Columbian Exposition' held in Chicago in 1893.*

for instance, was attended by tens of thousands, not least Queen Victoria herself in May 1887, as part of her Golden Jubilee celebrations. Like many of its predecessors, it was held in a specially constructed iron-and-glass arena. Its principal attraction was, uniquely, 'Buffalo' Bill Cody's 'Wild West' show with Annie Oakley, which included displays of 'fancy riding' and 'sharp-shooting'.

Originally derelict land by the railway, the Earl's Court site used by Buffalo Bill became a regular venue for popular exhibitions and entertainments. Not least among them was the 'The Great Wheel', a giant Ferris Wheel erected in 1895. Three-quarters the size of the modern London Eye, the Great Wheel was a familiar London landmark until it was demolished in 1907. Now the area houses the Earl's Court Exhibition Centre, which was built in 1937.

MUSEUMS

Another time I heard a matron say, "We're a-goin' to the British Museum this year, though South Kensington's a deal better. There can't be no comparison. If you know anythink about anythink, you're bound to enj'y yerself there."

RICHARD ROWE, *LIFE IN THE LONDON STREETS*, 1881

Of course, long before the Great Exhibition was conceived, traditional museums were a feature of the nineteenth-century tourist's itinerary. The grandest was the British Museum, which originally housed the private collection of a physician, Sir Hans Sloane. The collection was bought by Parliament upon Sloane's death in 1753, making the United Kingdom the first

Opposite: The cathedral-like Central Hall of the Natural History Museum is just one element of Alfred Waterhouse's ornate Romanesque design. The museum opened in 1881.

Below: The British Museum's famous domed Reading Room was built between 1854 and 1857. It now forms part of the redesigned Great Court and is open to the public.

country to invest in such a cultural resource for the benefit of the general public. It contained everything from classical antiquities, coins, prints and drawings, to zoological and fossil collections (the latter being relocated to the Natural History Museum in the 1880s). The museum also housed a vast library, and was legally entitled to receive a copy of any book published in the United Kingdom. The book collection was removed to the British Library in St Pancras in 1997, but the famous circular Reading Room, which opened in 1857, still remains.

The Museum District

Nothing rivalled the British Museum until the second half of the nineteenth century, when the South Kensington museums – today's Victoria & Albert Museum, Natural History Museum and Science Museum – were founded. These were, in fact, by-products of the Great Exhibition. The commissioners of the exhibition, with enthusiastic support from Prince Albert, had ploughed their profits into the purchase of land south of Hyde Park, with a view to creating one or more permanent institutions to house items purchased from the exhibition and to promote excellence in art and industry.

The first such institution on the site was the Museum of Manufactures, which opened in 1857. It was later renamed the South Kensington Museum, and eventually became the Victoria and Albert Museum – popularly known today as the V&A – when the foundation stone of the present building was laid by Queen Victoria in 1899.

In 1881, the Natural History Museum opened on adjoining ground that had formerly been the site of the 1862

Above: The Tate Britain, formerly known as the Tate Gallery, on Millbank was gifted to the nation by sugar magnate Henry Tate in 1894 to house his art collection, which he had already bequeathed some years earlier.

International Exhibition. It is a magnificent terracotta-clad building, replete with intricate carvings of animals and plants.

The Science Museum, meanwhile, was formed when the scientific collections of the V&A were separated out in 1885, though the present building was not opened until 1928. Needless to say, this trio has remained consistently popular, and both the V&A and Science Museum still contain many of the items that were shown at the Great Exhibition itself.

Individual Collections

Many Victorian tourists got no further than the British Museum or, in the second half of the century, the delights of South Kensington. Then as now, one might spend a whole day in any one of these great museums and not be disappointed. There were, however, a number of smaller museums in the Victorian capital, which were either private collections or the property of learned societies. The majority have long since disappeared, including a number subsumed by the developments at Kensington.

There was, for instance, a museum associated with the East India Company. This closed in 1865 following the company's demise, and its contents proceeded, via the India Office, to parts of the V&A, British Museum and Kew Gardens. Likewise, both the Patent Office Museum and Museum of Practical Geology in Jermyn Street eventually became part of the Science Museum.

Other museums and galleries simply declined in popularity and closed, such as Miss Linwood's Gallery of Needlework, a permanent exhibition of needlework art. The display ran for over thirty years, until it closed in 1845, having made Miss Linwood a wealthy woman.

Personal Bequests

A handful of these small collections, however, have survived to the present day. The most fascinating example, albeit originating before the Victorian period, but most certainly visited by Victorians, is to be found in the house of Sir John Soane (1753–1837), the architect of the Bank of England. Situated in Lincoln's Inn Fields, the house has never been that well known to the public, and, indeed, it is easy to walk past without noticing it. Yet it contains a highly idiosyncratic collection of antiquities, curiosities and paintings scattered among twenty-four rooms, from an Egyptian sarcophagus in the basement to William Hogarth's famous series of pictures, *A Rake's Progress* (1735).

Soane left his house to the nation upon his death in 1837, having negotiated an Act of Parliament that ensured its preservation. The agreement contained a proviso that the contents remain, as much as possible, in the arrangement in which he left them – thus we can still view the house today, precisely as Victorian visitors did a century and a half before us.

Another remarkable nineteenth-century bequest – the Wallace Collection – can be found in Manchester Square, a mile or so west of Lincoln's Inn. This is a fine collection of paintings, porcelain, furniture and an amazing assembly of suits of armour. It was left to the nation by Lady Wallace in 1897, with the request that the contents be 'unmixed with other objects of art'. The museum opened in 1900.

A similar, even grander example of Victorian philanthropy, by the sugar magnate Henry Tate, is also worth a mention. Tate gave his art collection to the nation in 1890, and built the Tate Gallery (now Tate Britain) on Millbank to house it.

OPTICAL ILLUSIONS

THE ORIGINAL DIORAMA, Regent's Park – NOW EXHIBITING, two highly interesting Pictures, each 70 feet broad and 50 feet high, representing MOUNT AETNA in SICILY, DURING an ERUPTION, and the ROYAL CASTLE of STOLZENFELS on the RHINE, with various effects. – Admission to both pictures only 1s; children under 12 years, half price. Open from 10 til dusk.

ADVERTISEMENT FROM *DAILY NEWS*, APRIL 1851

If museums and exhibitions provided, excluding Buffalo Bill, a rather sedate and educational experience for the tourist, there were other more dramatic London 'sights'. In particular, long before the invention of the modern cinema, or even the photograph, nineteenth-century Londoners were already sitting in darkened rooms and looking at pictures – this was the world of the 'panorama' and 'diorama'.

Early Inventions
Both panorama and diorama, in fact, predate the Victorian era. The panorama was the invention of artist Robert Barker. Barker came up with a system of warping perspective in a painting and then placing

Above: John Soane's eclectic collection includes paintings by Hogarth, Reynolds, Turner, et al.; specimens of Roman and Greek architecture; and the sarcophagus of Seti I of Egypt.

the picture on a cylindrical surface to give a 360-degree 'panoramic' view to those standing in the centre of the cylinder. He opened the first example, the Leicester Square Panorama, in 1793. After Barker's death in 1806, his exhibition was kept open by a Mr Burford, and in the 1840s it cost a shilling to see 'two views of celebrated places'. The building finally closed in 1865.

A rival panorama had opened in 1827 at the Colosseum, a rather grand building close to Regent's Park. Resembling the Pantheon in Rome, the Colosseum also contained conservatories, a Gothic aviary, a 'Temple of Theseus' and a 'Swiss Cottage'. Its panorama featured London rooftops, based on the view from St Paul's Cathedral, and survived until 1875 when the building was demolished.

The diorama was developed a little later, the invention of Louis-Jacques-Mandé Daguerre (1789–1851),

Coloſseum, Regents Park, London.

who would later produce the 'dageurreotype' system of photography. The London Diorama opened in 1823, also near to Regent's Park. Essentially, lighting and other effects were skilfully applied to sections of a large painted scene, which might be anything from the interior of Canterbury Cathedral to the eruption of Mount Etna. The audience, meanwhile, sat in a darkened room, observing the spectacle. The London Diorama included a rotating platform, on which the audience could be turned round to view a second painting. It survived until 1852 when the building was converted into a Baptist chapel.

The Leicester Square Tradition

Another similar tourist attraction, though not quite an optical illusion, was Wyld's Great Globe in the centre of Leicester Square, which opened in 1851 to cash in on the crowds drawn to the Great Exhibition. Sixty feet in diameter, visitors would progress through its four gas-lit floors, looking at the 'physical features of the earth' portrayed on its inner surface. It was demolished in 1861.

Leicester Square was also home to Saville House, until its destruction by fire in 1865. This was a sort of Victorian 'multiplex', consiting of assorted exhibition rooms and entertainment areas. At one point or another it not only housed panoramas, but freak shows, magic shows, scientific lectures, *poses plastiques* (live models in flesh-coloured body stockings acting as 'human statues' on stage), Miss Linwood's Gallery of Needlework, plus a billiards room and a shooting gallery.

The Victorians were, in fact, great enthusiasts for visual spectacle. We think of the twentieth century as a visual age with moving pictures, television and glossy magazines; but in the nineteenth century people were remarkably eager to see foreign places, natural wonders, dramatic events. And special effects or spectacular subject matter were not prerequisites: for example, thousands flocked to the Royal Academy of Arts to see William Frith's panoramic painting *The Railway Station* in 1862, eager to gaze upon an accurate representation of everyday life: a busy platform at Paddington Station, which was painted on a giant canvas.

Above: Photographers knew it paid to advertise, and many were former painters, in particular miniaturists, whom the new art of photography had made redundant.

New Visual Delights

Panoramas and dioramas did not really survive the 1860s, however, as other startling visual delights began to take their place. On a small scale, photography was becoming commonplace; Londoners had been able to obtain dageurreotype photographs of themselves from the early 1840s onwards, but by the

Below: A popular optical illusion at the Polytechnic Institution was 'Pepper's Ghost', which utilized a reflection in angled glass to give the impression of a ghostly presence.

1860s new methods of photography made portraits quicker and cheaper to take, and photographers' studios were soon dotted throughout London.

Above: Astley's Amphitheatre on Westminster Bridge Road was an unusual London theatre in that it was built round a circus ring, which was used for equestrian displays.

Opposite: Her Majesty's Theatre, Haymarket was destroyed by fire in 1867, rebuilt, then demolished in 1891 due to commercial failure. The present building dates from 1897.

Victorian optical devices for the home were also increasingly available, such as stereoscopic photography, which provided three-dimensional effects if one looked at specially prepared photographs through a viewing device. Magic lanterns, which were essentially slide projectors, also came into their own. Improvements in lantern design allowed public showings where images were projected onto screens twenty or thirty feet wide.

The most famous venue for such shows was the Polytechnic Institution in Regent Street, an educational institution showcasing 'popular science'. Among

other things, visitors to the institution could submerge themselves in a diving bell. Although a 'scientific' establishment, it hosted many entertainments. In particular, during the 1860s, the Polytechnic was the venue for 'Pepper's Ghost', an optical illusion in which, through careful use of projection and angled glass, an apparition appeared to walk across a stage. Needless to say, this proved a major attraction.

These and many other Victorian optical devices and amusements were precursors to a dramatic development that would change the nature of 'sight-seeing'. In 1896 the first demonstrations of the Kinetic Camera, Theatrograph and Cinematographe were given in London at various locations, including the Polytechnic in Regent Street – five years before the reign of Victoria ended, the modern cinema was born.

THEATRE AND MUSIC HALL

Look around you, in the vast arena of Her Majesty's. Wonder and admire… this magnificent theatre, glorious with beauties and with riches. Here are gathered the mighty, and noble, and wealthy, the venerable and wise, the young and beauteous of the realm. The prime minister seeks at the opera a few hours' relaxation from the toils of office; the newly-married peeress there displays the dazzling diamonds custom now, for the first time, permits her to wear; the blushing maiden of seventeen, "just out"—that very day, perhaps, presented at Court—smiles and simpers in a shrine of gauze and artificial flowers. Mark yonder, that roomy box on the grand tier, which a quiet, plainly-dressed party has just entered. There is a matronly lady in black… the matronly lady is Victoria Queen of England, and the middle-aged gentleman, inclined to corpulence and baldness, is his Royal Highness the Prince Consort.

GEORGE SALA, *TWICE ROUND THE CLOCK*, 1859

If the panorama, diorama and so on were novelties, best suited to occasional visits from tourists, then cinema was initially considered in much the same way. If the average Londoner looked anywhere for an evening's entertainment, it was the theatre.

Stage Law

At the beginning of Victoria's reign, the London stage was divided between the two 'patent' theatres of Drury Lane and Covent Garden – which had the historical right to produce drama – and all other theatres, which did not have such rights. These other theatres were, in fact, obliged to include music as part of any entertainment, lest it be judged a drama by the licensing authorities; hence comic operas and musical farce were the norm.

Most of these theatres, moreover, had a reputation for rowdy audiences; they were not, by and large, places to which a respectable gentleman might take his wife. The exception to this rule was Her Majesty's Opera House on the Haymarket, which was the principal venue for opera in the metropolis; it was good enough for royalty and featured the leading performers of the day.

The theatrical scene in London changed, however, in 1843 when the Theatre Regulation Act abolished the distinction between 'patent' theatres and the rest. It freed up London's theatres for respectable dramatists, allowing, for example, the team of Mr and Mrs Charles Kean to produce nine years of Shakespearian revivals at the Princess's Theatre on Oxford Street during the 1850s. The 1843 act also prohibited drinking in any licensed auditorium, while allowing it in saloon theatres (small venues attached to public houses) and supper rooms. Thus it inadvertently helped to foster a new type of theatrical experience – 'music hall'.

Cheap Entertainment

Music-hall entertainment – a line-up of alternating singers, dancers, magicians, comedians et al. – was unknown in the early 1840s. However, there were various types of entertainment that prefigured it.

There were informal 'harmonic meetings', where men from a particular workplace or charitable association would gather in a pub to drink and sing songs. A chairman (probably the most senior member of the group) organized the event and each man might do a 'turn', perhaps interspersed with the contribution of a local professional singer known to the publican.

There were also more formally arranged 'song and supper rooms', where food and drink was served and professional singers, often comic, were engaged.

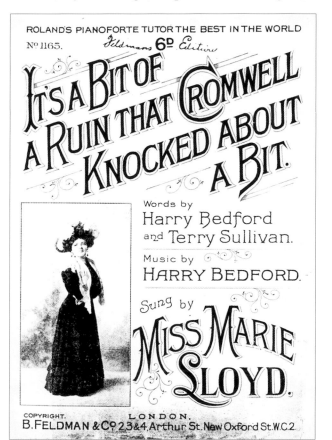

Above: Marie Lloyd was among the most popular music-hall performers. Her repertoire included saucy numbers, such as What's That For, eh?.

These included, in the 1840s, the Coal-Hole on the Strand, Cyder Cellars on Maiden Lane and Evan's on King Street, all in the vicinity of Covent Garden. In such places the food was plain and the atmosphere cosmopolitan and boisterous, catering to 'flash' young men and students.

Finally, there were 'penny gaffs': these were makeshift spaces that served as improvised theatres for the poor, presenting racy melodrama and cheap entertainment of all sorts; many of them were attached to pubs.

A Raging Success

The 1843 act gave a choice to publicans who had previously used such shows to draw in crowds: either to present teetotal drama or alcohol-fuelled music. Most, of course, chose the latter. Some enterprising individuals actually resolved to extend the meeting rooms and improvised theatre spaces they had previously made available to the public. Gradually, these spaces became theatres attached to the pubs, which were otherwise known as music halls. Professional 'chairmen' were introduced to manage proceedings and book professional acts, and a circuit of halls offering regular work developed.

FAMOUS ENTERTAINERS IN VICTORIAN LONDON

Lottie Collins

Ta-ra-ra-boom-de-ay, which was first performed at the Tivoli Music Hall in 1891.

Henry Irving (1838–1905)
Shakespearean actor and manager of the Lyceum Theatre 1878–99.

Dan Leno (1860–1904)
Music-hall performer who starred in pantomimes at the Drury Lane Theatre throughout the 1890s.

Jules Leotard (1838–70)
The original 'Daring Young Man on the Flying Trapeze' performed at Cremorne Gardens, Chelsea in the 1860s.

Jenny Lind (1820–87)
'The Swedish Nightingale' soprano made her London debut in 1847 at Her Majesty's Theatre, attracting huge crowds.

Marie Lloyd (1870–1922)
Music-hall performer, famous for her suggestive performances. She made her debut at the Eagle Tavern on City Road in 1885.

William Charles Macready (1793–1873)
Actor-manager who gave his final performance, as Macbeth, at the Drury Lane Theatre in 1851.

Ellen Terry

John Nevil Maskelyne (1839–1917)
Magician who performed with his partner George Cooke at the Egyptian Hall from 1873 to 1904.

Ellen Terry (1848–1928)
Leading Shakespearean actress who performed in Henry Irving's company at the Lyceum.

'Zazel' (Rosa Richter) (1860–1937)
The original 'human canonball', whose first performance was at the Royal Aquarium in 1877.

Blondin (1824–97)
The French tightrope walker who crossed Niagara Falls and gave performances at the Crystal Palace in the 1860s. He was buried at Kensal Green Cemetery.

Buffalo Bill (William F. Cody; 1846–1917)
Wild West showman who performed in London in 1887 as part of Queen Victoria's Golden Jubilee.

Lottie Collins (1865–1910)
Music-hall performer who gained national fame with the song

Acts would dash around London, starring at several venues in one night.

The first substantial music hall was the Canterbury in Lambeth. Constructed in 1852, it was rebuilt on a larger scale two years later and again in the 1870s. Indeed, so successful did the best variety acts become that, in time, the association with existing public houses disappeared entirely and halls were built for their own sake.

By the end of the century, music hall was a clearly defined business, with its own stars such as Marie Lloyd and Dan Leno, who were not only famous in London but nationally. Unlike mainstream theatres, however, which had become increasingly respectable, music hall stayed a little closer to its decidedly working-class roots, even as lavish new halls were built throughout the country. Drink was always on tap and the entertainment was often rather risqué, relying on the British love of puns and innuendo. Marie Lloyd, for instance, reportedly enjoyed singing songs like *She'd Never Had Her Ticket Punched Before* in two styles – one performance made the meaning very clear, the other she reserved for the licensing authorities that oversaw public morality.

PARKS

*Let an Englishman make a park, and his
production will be admirable.*

MAX SCHLESINGER, *SAUNTERINGS IN AND ABOUT
LONDON*, 1853

Not all sights in Victorian London were indoor amusements. In particular, the metropolis contained numerous parks and green spaces. These broadly fell into two categories. The central London parks of Green Park, Hyde Park, Kensington Gardens, Regent's Park and St James's Park were 'Royal Parks' – tracts of land acquired by various English monarchs and then opened to the public; their historical importance and central location made them a traditional haunt of tourists. Suburban parks, on the other hand, were largely a product of Victoria's reign. These swathes of green, such as Victoria Park in east London, were

purchased by government from private individuals for the benefit of the public. The intention was to provide 'lungs' for the smoke-ridden city and to guarantee some open space for 'rational recreation' – as opposed to the traditional recreations of drinking and gambling.

There is always, of course, an interesting exception: Alexandra Park in Hornsey, north London, was originally laid out as a commercial speculation to rival the development of the Crystal Palace gardens at Sydenham in south-east London. In a direct parallel, the central attraction at Hornsey was the Alexandra Palace, which opened in 1873 and was a reconstruction of the 1862 International Exhibition building at Kensington. Alexandra Palace, however, never proved as successful as its southern competitor, not least because the first palace burnt down two weeks after it opened, taking two more years to rebuild. Indeed, following prolonged commercial failure, ownership was ultimately transferred to local government in 1900. Today Alexandra Palace is a multi-purpose venue.

Park Activities

What did the Victorians do in their parks? Much like today, they could stroll past bandstands, boating lakes and landscaped gardens, but some attractions were unique to particular locations. In Hyde Park, for instance, a visitor might watch the parade of fashionable carriages along Rotten Row in the summer, while in the winter indulge in ice-skating on the park's frozen lake, the Serpentine.

In Regent's Park, he or she might visit London Zoo, or rather the 'Zoological Gardens', which were founded by the Zoological Society in 1826 for the 'introduction and exhibition of the Animal Kingdom alive or properly preserved', where both children and adults could take rides on the elephants. South London's Battersea Park, meanwhile, became the place for observing the antics

Left: Alexandra Palace in Muswell Hill, north London, was an ill-fated rival to the Crystal Palace. Its first incarnation opened for only sixteen days in 1873 before being destroyed by fire; it reopened in 1875.

of cyclists, a fashionable pursuit during the mid-1890s. St James's Park even boasted a small number of cows, which were able to provide fresh milk.

The parks were also home to less salubrious activities. In the late evening, locations such as Hyde Park and Green Park were a notorious haunt of prostitutes. They also provided an overnight refuge for the homeless, and it was not uncommon to see poor children washing themselves in the Serpentine early in the morning. To counter such antisocial activity, Hyde Park boasted its own police station of thirty policemen.

Parks, however, generally had a good reputation. The opening of a suburban park was seen to benefit both public health – by creating a clean open space for the public to exercise – and public morals, by creating a space where a working man might take his family on a Sunday rather than spending his time in a pub.

Right: The Gothic drinking fountain in Victoria Park, east London, was donated by the philanthropist Angela Burdett-Coutts to promote health and temperance among park-goers.

Below: The Coalbrookdale Gates are the last trace of the 1851 Great Exhibition in Hyde Park. They were displayed at the exhibition as an example of British craftsmanship.

Above: St James's Park, with its ornamental lake and rare birds, was famously popular with nursemaids and their infant charges.

It is an odd fact, therefore, that when Victoria came to the throne, there were similar suburban green spaces throughout London, which many Victorians were keen to abolish, and all of which disappeared during Victoria's reign – London's 'Pleasure Gardens'.

PLEASURE GARDENS

To attempt a description of the numerous and varied sources of entertainment at this unrivalled establishment would be vain. Concert in the open air, dancing and vaudeville in the Saloon, set paintings, cosmoramas, fountains, grottos, elegant buildings, arcade, colonnade, grounds, statuary, singing, music, &c.; render it a fairy scene, of which a due estimate can only be formed by inspection. Open every evening… Admission 2s.

ADVERTISEMENT FOR THE EAGLE TAVERN PLEASURE GROUND, 1838

Pleasure gardens were out-of-town commercial ventures built for public recreation that could often trace their roots to the late seventeenth or eighteenth century. Many were simply small-scale landscaped gardens, often created by the enterprising proprietor of a public house to attract customers. The gardens of the Eagle Tavern on City Road, east London, were a well-known, above-average example. Some were on an even bigger scale, with extensive grounds built around spas or tea-rooms; others little more than a plot of grass.

Most of the smaller gardens disappeared during the nineteenth century, to be replaced by housing as London's suburbs expanded. However, three particularly large and notable examples survived into the Victorian era: Vauxhall Gardens, which first opened in 1661; Bagnigge Wells, near King's Cross, which opened *c.* 1690; and Cremorne Gardens in Chelsea, a late arrival that opened in 1832.

These large gardens were undoubtedly quite spectacular in their day, laid out in carefully cultivated tree-lined avenues, with covered walkways, arbours and statuary. Each contained some striking pieces of outdoor architecture, such as pagodas and rotundas,

Above: In addition to lions and tigers, famous attractions at London Zoo included Obaysch, the first hippopotamus to be seen in Europe since Roman times (resident 1850–78), and Jumbo the elephant (resident 1865–82).
Right: Jules Leotard, inventor of the flying trapeze and after whose costume the 'leotard' is named, dazzled audiences at Chelsea's Cremorne Gardens in the 1860s.

which often furnished a location for dancing, concerts or other kinds of live musical and theatrical performance. By the nineteenth century, they also regularly provided a location for fireworks and balloon ascents.

The Decline of the Pleasure Garden

Unfortunately, by the time Victoria came to the throne, both Vauxhall and Bagnigge Wells seemed less attractive than they once had been. In part, this was simply a question of badly maintained buildings and grounds. Charles Dickens, writing in *Sketches by Boz* of a tour of Vauxhall in 1836, declared that he 'met with a disappointment at every turn', encountering peeling paintwork, dingy ornamentation and gloomy walks.

In part, however, pleasure gardens were associated in the public mind with immorality, perceived as

Above: Despite its impressive appearance, The Eagle Tavern Pleasure Ground in City Road was described in 1850 as 'frequented by the lower orders'.

Opposite: Tennis was championed by the All-England Croquet Club, who started competitions at Wimbledon in 1877. Croquet soon took second place to the new sport.

belonging to an earlier, more louche era. Many were convinced that their groves and night-time entertainment provided ideal places for concealing outdoor prostitution.

Nevertheless, Vauxhall's entertainments continued for a further twenty years after Dickens's visit. Max Schlesinger, a German writer who published an account of his travels in London, noted a programme in 1853 that included 'music, singing, horsemanship, illuminations, dancing, rope-dancing, acting, comic songs, hermits, gipsies, and fireworks'. The gardens finally closed in 1859. Bagnigge Wells, in turn, had already closed in 1842, largely because of its location – originally a pleasant retreat on the borders of London, it had gradually become surrounded on all sides by Islington's suburban housing developments.

By the 1860s, the only large pleasure gardens in London that survived were Cremorne Gardens in Chelsea. On a typical night in 1861, visitors stepping off a steamboat on the Thames could witness Jules Leotard, the world's first trapeze artist; Mr D'Alberte, a rope-walker; a singer; a concert; a pantomime; a 'celebrated circus troupe of educated dogs and monkeys'; Signor Core, 'The Italian Salamander, or Fire King'; and a 'grand display of fireworks' – all for one shilling! But, by the 1870s, the gardens were under constant attack from all sides: complaints by local residents about noise and trouble-makers, moralists concerned about prostitution, and speculative builders who thought they could make better use of the land. Endless debates about the licensing of the gardens came to a head in 1877, when they finally closed for good.

The gardens at the Eagle Tavern survived into the 1880s; but the tavern itself, having succeeded for a while as a theatre offering spectacular melodramas, became unprofitable. It was sold in 1884 to the Salvation Army.

SPORT

Lawn tennis. – Of modern inventions in the way of games, this is one of the best. It is suitable to young and middle-aged men and women. It has many advantages over other ball games, as it can be played at home with one's own friends; it may be engaged in for a variable length of time; it can be taken up with safety by anyone without previous training; it is less likely to give rise to serious accidents than other ball games. Lawn tennis has more adherents than has cricket; it includes men, women and children among its devotees. As pursued in towns exercise of this kind is not in the 'highest' sense beneficial, as it is performed in a polluted ozoneless air. Still, as stated previously, exercise taken in even such an atmosphere as that of a London park, or a garden in a square, is better than none at all.

JAMES CANTLIE, DEGENERATION AMONGST LONDONERS, 1885

The Victorians' enthusiasm for parks and 'rational recreation' extended to sport, and they indulged in a similar range of sports to those we enjoy today. Cricket was the well-established 'national sport', with grounds in London at the Oval in south London (purchased in 1845), Lord's in St John's Wood (laid out in 1814), both of which still exist today, plus smaller pitches such as the 'Prince's Cricket Ground' in Sloane Square, which flourished in the 1870s.

Lawn Tennis, on the other hand, was a Victorian invention, although based on racket games that had existed for centuries. A Major Walter Wingfield created it in 1873, as a less sedate alternative to the traditional game of croquet. Wingfield dubbed the game 'Sphairistike or Lawn Tennis' and sold patented tennis kits, which were an immense success. There was, however, little point in the new game remaining patented once it became popular, as anyone could acquire a racket and improvise a net. When the patent lapsed, the All England Croquet Club ran a men's tennis singles championship at Wimbledon in 1877, which has continued to this day. The Lawn Tennis Association, the sport's governing body, was formed in 1888.

Below: Cricket was the best-established sport in Victorian London, with two dedicated grounds: Lord's, shown here, which was acquired in 1816, and the Oval, acquired in 1845.

Above: The team sport of football grew significantly during the Victorian era, with many of today's clubs having their origins in workers' clubs or school clubs.

The Growth of Sporting Associations

Many other sports of the period, although not Victorian in origin, were systematized and regulated by newly created national associations in the second half of the nineteenth century. Football is the prime example, with the Football Association (F.A.), which formed in London in 1863 and whose eleven founding members included teams drawn from the Civil Service and Charterhouse School. The first national F.A. Cup was held in 1871–2 and a national Football League ran in 1888. Many modern London football clubs can also trace their history back to the Victorian period: Arsenal, for instance, has its roots in the 'Dial Square' club formed by workers at the Woolwich Arsenal in 1886.

Other governing bodies formed in the late Victorian period include the Amateur Boxing Association in 1880, the Amateur Athletic Club in 1866, and the Rugby Football Union in 1871. Cricket is a notable absentee from the list, as its rules were already well established by the mid-eighteenth century. The most shocking development in cricket in the Victorian era was, rather, the first defeat of England by Australia at the Oval in 1882.

Illegal Pastimes

Of course, not all Victorian sports were well-organized team games. Illegal sports flourished in the first half of the century. Prize-fights, in particular, were held at secret locations, allowing unlicensed gambling. Crowd trouble was commonplace, especially if such events were raided by the police. The acceptance of the Marquess of Queensbury rules, however, in the late 1860s, and a growing distrust of 'fixed' matches, put paid to big illicit prizefights.

Above: Bicycle races regularly took place at the purpose-built cycle track of the south London Herne Hill Velodrome in the 1890s; the track survives to this day.

Likewise, although the term may be a misnomer, 'blood sports' were very popular. Cock-fighting, dog-fighting and rat-killing contests attracted crowds who often included not only the poor, but 'flash' members of the aristocracy, who enjoyed the company of 'sportsmen' (that is, the opportunity for placing a bet). However, as Victorian society grew more orderly and better policed, the following for blood sports diminished.

There were other metropolitan sports associated with gaming, and the capital contained many billiard rooms, ranging from rather exclusive establishments patronized by the wealthy, to those in seedy public houses. A good number of pubs also had skittle grounds or, from the 1860s, the more fashionable American-style bowling alleys, in their cellars and out-buildings.

Sporting Choice

Outdoors, there were healthier alternatives: angling was popular among the working classes, along both the River Lea and the capital's network of canals; the Thames was used for rowing matches, not least the famous Oxford and Cambridge Boat Race which began in 1829; bicycle races were organized from the 1870s onwards; swimming races took place in the Thames and the Serpentine during the summer, and in public baths in winter; athletic contests were held at suburban sports grounds; even golf was played in areas such as Blackheath, home of the long-established Royal Blackheath Golf Club.

Women, however, were not really expected to participate in sport, or at least nothing that required working up a sweat. At best, some magazines recommend calisthenics (gentle aerobics) in the home and tennis was a possibility once it became established (Wimbledon's women's championships began in 1884, with merely 13 players). Wealthier women could also indulge in horse-riding or archery: the Royal Toxophilite Society was established in the Inner Circle of Regent's Park in 1832, and there were other clubs in London, plus archery grounds at the Crystal Palace in Sydenham at which national contests were held.

And, although not essentially a sport, it is perhaps worth noting that there was a craze for roller-skating in the 1870s, and bicycling in the 1890s, which at least allowed women a modicum of vigorous exercise. Not everyone approved of women having such freedom, however, and many commentators complained vociferously about the unchaperoned activities of both skaters and 'lady bicyclists'.

FOOD AND DRINK

EDIBLES

Dining is the privilege of civiliza-tion. The rank which a people occupy in the grand scale may be measured by their way of taking their meals, as well as by their way of treating their women. The nation which knows how to dine has learnt the leading lesson of progress.

MRS BEETON'S BOOK OF HOUSEHOLD MANAGEMENT, 1861

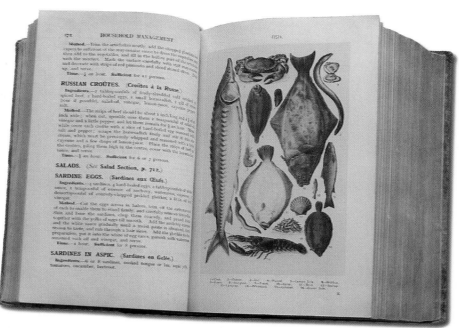

What did Londoners eat in the 19th century? For a middle-class family, a typical breakfast would probably include bread and butter, bacon and eggs, not unlike the 'cooked breakfast' still popular throughout modern Britain. It was also expected that some form of cooked meat would be on offer, perhaps sausages, chops or kidneys, but more often fish, such as haddock or mackerel. Another favourite addition was a selection of cold cuts, whose flavour might be enhanced by a bottled sauce, such as anchovy paste, a popular Victorian relish.

Later in the day, luncheon might incorporate 'cold joints, nicely garnished, a few sweets, or a little hashed meat, poultry or game... with bread and cheese, biscuits, butter, &c.', to quote Mrs Beeton's famous book of recipes and advice, with rump-steak, kidneys, chops or cutlets for those with a greater appetite.

Mrs Beeton's Menus

It was the evening meal, however, that was the 'grand solid meal of the day'. A dinner at home would typi-cally consist of three courses: fish or soup, meat and vegetables, and dessert. *Mrs Beeton's Book of Household Management* helpfully provided a set of menu suggestions for 'plain family dinners', listed month by month to suit seasonal food-stuffs, which give a good indication of the middle-class diet of the time.

Most remarkable is the variety of meat and fish. The fish on Mrs Beeton's 'plain' menus included turbot, whiting, sole, salmon, brill and lobster. Meat dishes included mutton, leg of pork, rib of beef, pheasant, rabbit, roast chicken, rump-steak, calf's-head, roast lamb, stewed knuckle of veal, calf's liver, roast duck and roast hare. Indeed, it is only the

Above: Isabella Beeton (1836–65) was a best-selling author. Her Book of Household Management, *published 1859–61, sold two million copies by the end of the 1860s.*

Opposite: Rules Restaurant in Maiden Lane, Covent Garden, was founded in 1798. Famous for its oysters, it was a favourite of both Charles Dickens and the Prince of Wales.

desserts that seem a little monotonous today – heavy puddings and stewed fruit predominated, plum pud-ding being a favourite, occasionally leavened by the inclusion of pancakes, tarts, semolina or blancmange.

Of course, not every middle-class home, even in the fashion-conscious metropolis, followed the dictates of Mrs Beeton, sampling a fresh recipe every night. Diet varied according to personal taste and income, and some Victorians also took an interest in nutrition. Indeed, there was a small but vociferous vegetarian movement, which began with the founda-tion of the national Vegetarian Society in 1848. A rival organization, the London Vegetarian Society, was founded in 1888, and numbered the young Mahatma Gandhi among its members. Likewise, the present trend for low-carbohydrate diets can trace its origins to William Banting's *Letter on Corpulence*, which was published in 1869. Written by a London cabinet-maker, the book was so successful that, for many years, the verb 'banting' was a synonym for dieting.

Above: Vegetarianism was a bizarre notion to many Victorians, and an easy target for the satirical magazine Punch, *as can be seen in this cartoon from 1852.*

Good Home Cooking

The Victorians had a fairly different relationship with food to that experienced by most people today. For one, most meals in middle-class homes were entirely home-made, prepared by the household's cook. It was possible to obtain good ready-made meals from the local baker or pastry-cook, especially if catering for a large dinner-party, but such arrangements were frowned upon.

The Victorians also had a particular reverence for 'plain cooking' – simple boiling or roasting of meat and avoiding the use of rich sauces – and an abhorrence of waste and extravagance. Leftovers would generally be recycled into the following day's dish. *Cassell's Household Guide*, an 1870s household manual, even begins its cookery section with the advice: 'Everybody knows that a good cook is an economical cook… Save every bone, every leaf, every crust, and make them into soup, if not for your own children, for the children of those poorer than yourself.'

This may sound condescending to a modern reader, but certainly many among the London poor would have been grateful for such handouts. The lower classes had much less choice in their diet. In fact, it was often more a question of finding something that was remotely edible in the first place.

INEDIBLES

I have already spoken of the difficulty in guessing what can be the food on which these people live, and the sties, cowsheds, and slaughter-houses suggest to the inquiring mind a terrible association with the large number of shops where the coarsest parts of meat seem to share the space with what butchers call offal. Cow-heels, bullocks'-hearts, kidneys, and livers, thin and poor-looking tripe, and sheeps-heads… piles and chains of bruised, and often damaged-looking, saveloys, black-puddings, and a sort of greasy cakes of baked sausage-meat, known as 'faggots,' sold for a penny or three farthings…

THOMAS ARCHER, *THE PAUPER, THE THIEF AND THE CONVICT*, 1865

Right: A costermonger in the slum district of Seven Dials sells herring at a penny or half-penny each, according to size. The poor bought much of their food from street vendors.

One of the greatest problems facing the lower classes in London was the quality of their food. This was a two-fold difficulty: firstly, many could not afford decent food, particularly meat, and so relied on poor-quality fare; secondly, until public health legislation was passed in the 1870s, many of the staples of the working-class diet were either contaminated by unhygienic conditions or adulterated by unscrupulous suppliers. Bread, in particular, was notorious for being bulked-out by anything bakers could lay their hands on, including rice and old potatoes, and doctored with alum and chalk to give it added whiteness.

Working-class Meals

This is not to say that anyone who could not afford Mrs Beeton's recipes existed on rations of stale bread and gruel. A family with access to a kitchen and where the father was in regular employment could probably expect a decent Sunday lunch. Thomas Wright describes one such meal in his 1867 book, *Some Habits and Customs of the Working Classes*; a dinner that includes leg of mutton, rabbit pie, apple pie and rice-pudding. Such lunches were, furthermore, as much a social ritual for the working class as dinners and dinner parties were for their betters, providing an opportunity to show off the finest crockery and wear 'Sunday best' clothing. Unlike in middle-class homes, however, a two- or three-course meal *only* appeared on the table of the artisan, factory worker or labourer on Sundays. The weekly expense was justified by the fact that it provided valuable nourishment for the breadwinner of the household.

Those who were not in regular paid employment were much less likely to see a decent joint of meat, not least because, in many cases, they had no cooking facilities in their lodgings. If they could occasionally afford a square meal, they were obliged to acquire the ingredients, then pay the local baker to cook it for them. For the poorest, in fact, home cookery was a luxury, quite irrelevant to their circumstances. They had to rely on snacks and cheap eateries – what we might call 'junk food' today – in other words, they were entirely dependent on eating out.

EATING OUT

The solids then, according to street estimation, consist of hot-eels, pickled whelks, oysters, sheep's-trotters, pea-soup, fried fish, ham-sandwiches, hot green peas, kidney puddings, boiled meat puddings, beef, mutton, kidney, and eel pies, and baked potatoes. In each of these provisions the street poor find a mid-day or midnight meal.

The pastry and confectionary which tempt the street eaters are tarts of rhubarb, currant, gooseberry, cherry, apple, damson, cranberry, and (so called) mince pies; plum dough and plum-cake; lard, currant, almond and many other varieties of cakes, as well as of tarts; gingerbread-nuts and heart-cakes; Chelsea buns; muffins and crumpets...

HENRY MAYHEW, *LONDON LABOUR AND THE LONDON POOR*, 1851

Henry Mayhew was a journalist who chronicled the lives of the poorest members of society in Victorian London, firstly in a series of articles for the *Morning Chronicle* newspaper (1849–50), then in book form in *London Labour and the London Poor*. Mayhew found a remarkably diverse range of cheap food being sold on the streets, both by itinerant vendors and from fixed stalls. Undoubtedly, some of it was not particularly nourishing, but it formed the staple diet of many who could not afford to cook for themselves.

This street fare, however, was merely the humblest way of 'eating out'. There were also many indoor venues where a man might obtain lunch or an evening meal, the quality of which depended on the size of his wallet.

Above: The baked-potato seller with his heated 'potato-can' and cry of 'Tatoes hot! – Penny a-piece – All hot! Hot! Hot!', was a common sight in London.

A Cheap Meal

The cheapest dining establishment was the humble 'cookshop', or 'soup-house', arguably the Victorian equivalent of the modern 'greasy spoon' café. Cookshop fare was very basic, only costing a penny or two, and included meals like pease-pudding, baked potatoes, 'ha'porths of pie-crust' (hot dough), saveloys, fried fish and soup. At its best, a local cookshop, typically in a slum district, supplied some basic nutrition.

A cut above the cookshop were dining-rooms. These largely catered to a lunchtime trade of clerks and businessmen in the City of London, and so were principally found around the districts of Bishopsgate, Fleet Street and Holborn. Some provided a written menu, in others the waiter read out what joints of

Below: Countless charities strived to offer support to the urban poor, and many found that soup kitchens were the best method of providing cheap basic nutrition to the masses.

meat were available. This was still quite plain fare, with a typical bill, according to *Knight's London*, 1842, being 'Meat 8d., potatoes 1d., bread 1d., cheese 1d.', but the meat was of much better quality than anything at a cookshop.

Serving a similar clientèle were '*à la mode* beef-houses', which specialized in a stew of beef and calves' feet, and provided a fast service as there was no choice beyond a 'four-penny plate' or 'six-penny plate'. Likewise, chop-houses specialized in mutton chops or steaks, as opposed to meat cut from hot joints as in the dining-rooms.

In the first half of the nineteenth century, many of these eateries also kept to the previous century's custom of offering an additional 'ordinary' – a set meal at a set price – at a particular time of day.

Right: The carefully renovated Victorian façade of the Quality Chop House in Farringdon hides a modern restaurant whose menu includes traditional jellied eels.

Below: Simpson's of Cornhill nests in a network of alleys opposite the Royal Exchange, and retains the traditional menu and shared benches of a Victorian dining-room.

Above: The George Inn in The Borough is London's last surviving galleried coaching inn. Such inns provided basic meals for travellers.

Pub Grub

Cooked food could also frequently be obtained at taverns (large public houses) and coaching inns, but the quality varied a good deal from place to place. Charles Dickens described the fare on offer at The Saracen's Head, a famous coaching-inn, in *Nicholas Nickleby* (1839) thus: 'large joints of roast and boiled, a tongue, a pigeon pie, a cold fowl, a tankard of ale, and other little matters of the like kind, which... are generally understood to belong more particularly to solid lunches, stage-coach dinners, or unusually substantial breakfasts.' The journalist George Sala, however, writing in 1859, described typical pub food as 'a pork pie, a sausage roll, and a Banbury cake'.

But what was distinctly lacking in London for much of the nineteenth century was anything resembling a modern restaurant. Anyone who sought 'continental cuisine' – the diametric opposite of the 'plain cookery' beloved by the English – had to betake to a select gentleman's club, a grand hotel or the bohemian delights of Soho, where a few French and Italian restaurant-cafés flourished, principally the resorts of European ex-patriates.

Where, then, did the modern London restaurant originate?

RESTAURANTS

Of late years there has been an attempt to change the eating-houses of Cheapside into pseudo "restaurants". Seductive announcements, brilliantly emblazoned, and showily framed and glazed, have been hung up, relating to "turtle" and "venison"; salmon, with wide waddling mouths, have gasped in the windows; and insinuating mural inscriptions have hinted at the existence of "Private dining-rooms for ladies". Now, whatever can ladies—though I have the authority of Mr. Charles Dibdin and my own lips for declaring that there are fine ones in the city— want to come and dine in Cheapside for?

GEORGE SALA, *TWICE ROUND THE CLOCK*, 1859

In the first half of the nineteenth century, decent women were not expected to dine out at all; their sphere was the home. In particular, chop-houses and public rooms at inns and taverns were masculine areas; any solitary woman lingering in such places would, likely as not, be assumed to be a prostitute. Private rooms were available, but were treated with a degree of suspicion.

It was not even the done thing for women to serve food in these masculine enclaves. In 1872 when Arthur Munby, a diarist famously obsessed with working women, found a staff of waitresses at a City restaurant, he declared it 'a wholesome innovation'. It was also a sign of the times, for the increased visibility of women in public was a feature of the second half of Victoria's reign, and, in turn, altered the nature of eating out.

Growing Demand

We can probably trace the demand for restaurants in London to the Great Exhibition and its successors, which drew huge 'mixed' crowds to London that had to be fed. It was soon realized that, when it came to catering for groups of men and women together, the few existing cafés, pastry-cook's shops and private rooms for ladies were plainly inadequate. On the other hand, the increasingly grand refreshment facilities offered at the exhibitions themselves showed what might be achieved.

Another agent for change in the 1860s and 1870s was that the West End theatres were becoming increasingly smart and respectable, and suitable for families. This fostered a demand for 'mixed' dining among a new breed of upper- and middle-class theatre-goers. Entrepreneurs even built joint restaurant and theatre developments, such as the Gaiety on the Strand, which opened in 1868, and the Criterion in Piccadilly, which opened in 1874, so that their clientèle had only to walk a few steps from table to auditorium. This, in turn, spurred on others who saw potential profits in West End restaurants.

Above: *The Criterion Restaurant and Theatre, Piccadilly, was opened in 1874 by Spiers and Pond, who were prominent railway caterers.*

In a parallel development, the growth in numbers of grand hotels – from those at railway termini, such as the Midland Grand at St Pancras, which opened in 1873, to The Savoy, which opened in 1889 – also created a vogue for dining out in style. These hotels invariably included attractive restaurants, exquisitely decorated and luxuriously furnished, and often had the best chefs in London.

All these factors combined to create a burgeoning restaurant culture in the metropolis. Indeed, by the mid-1890s, George Sala himself was painting a very different picture in a companion to *Twice Round the Clock* called *London Up to Date*. The world of fin de siècle London, Sala found, was one where 'chance diners' could telegraph or telephone a dinner reservation to their favourite hotel and eat together in comfort. Moreover, women could, if they chose, mingle with men in the hotel's smoking rooms – albeit only with their 'husbands and brothers' – before they departed for a night at theatre.

Admittedly, not everywhere was quite so enlightened, even by the end of the century. A few places clung to old customs, especially the fusty dining-rooms in the City. The author Arnold Bennett visited The Rainbow in Fleet Street in 1897 – 'a large dark room, sombrely furnished in mahogany, and gaslighted, even in the sunshine of a hot July day' – a place popular with lawyers and businessmen. Bennett found that women were not admitted to the ground floor, and any who dared go further than the private coffee-room 'would be requested to leave, or at least pointed at as unwomanly'. Nevertheless, The Rainbow and its ilk were fighting a rearguard action.

TEA AND COFFEE

Surely a pretty woman never looks prettier than when making tea. The most feminine and most domestic of all occupations imparts a magic harmony to her every movement, a witchery to her every glance.

MARY ELIZABETH BRADDON,
LADY AUDLEY'S SECRET, 1862

Another great advance for women in public life, in relation to eating and drinking, was struck in the late 1890s: the creation of London's tea-shops. There were, in fact, two rival chains that prospered at the end of the century: the A.B.C. (Aerated Bread Company) and J. Lyon's & Co. The precursors of modern fast-food franchises, the new tea-shops, serving tea and cakes, provided identical prices at each shop and relied on rigorous organization, presenting a thoroughly modern, hygienic, clean-cut image to the public. They were also, finally, commonplace, cheap, respectable places to which a single woman might go, by herself, for refreshment.

Afternoon Tea
J. Lyon's & Co.'s tea-shops and, later, grand 'corner house' restaurants, went on to dominate the capital in

Right: Simpson's-in-the-Strand has been serving food since the 1840s. The present dining-room opened in 1904, and is typical of grand restaurants of the early twentieth century.

Above: This late nineteenth-century building started out as the Angel coaching inn; it later became a Lyons tea-shop and now houses a bank.

Above: The Jerusalem Tavern in Clerkenwell was once a coffee-house; its renovated façade dates from the early nineteenth century.

the first half of twentieth century, only finally disappearing from London's high streets in the 1970s. Tea, however, was a popular beverage long before Lyon's appeared. It was first imported in bulk from China by the East India Company in the 1650s. By the nineteenth century, it was both the staple beverage of the poor, being relatively cheap and easy to prepare, and, following the vogue for taking 'afternoon tea' that started in the 1830s, it became the drink of choice for the wealthy.

Indeed, the demand for tea was actually such that, during the mid-nineteenth century, the British developed their own tea plantations in India (around Assam and Darjeeling and Ceylon), using the newly discovered Indian variety of the plant. Likewise, fast tea-clippers, such as the famous *Cutty Sark*, were built in the 1850s and 1860s specifically to speed up the tea-trade, with their captains competing to be the first to bring back the year's crop from China.

Coffee-Time

The alternative to tea was coffee. Associated in modern British minds with the continental espresso or the American import of Starbucks, coffee nevertheless has a long history in London. Coffee-houses first appeared in London in the mid-seventeenth century, and ironically also popularized the drinking of tea. They swiftly became fashionable meeting places for men about town, where they could exchange news or talk business. In fact, several of the City of London's great financial institutions, such as Lloyd's insurers and the Stock Exchange, were first established by eighteenth-century City brokers who congregated in particular coffee-houses. By the start of Victoria's reign, however, most of the more famous establishments had developed into exclusive gentlemen's clubs. The Victorian coffee-houses were generally of humbler origin, where, at best, manual workers or clerks might stop to take a drink and read a newspaper.

Coffee remained a popular beverage among the lower classes throughout the nineteenth century. It was sold on the streets at 'coffee stalls', which also offered tea or cocoa, bread and butter, sometimes even cakes or sandwiches. Some opened early in the morning to catch people on their way to work, others opened late into the night for the benefit of, as one writer put it, 'fast gentlemen and loose girls'. The stalls held one or more large tin cans of coffee, which were kept warm by charcoal burners, and customers would cluster round the stall, drinking from mugs supplied by the owner.

Tea and coffee also played an important social role in Victorian society, independent of their merits as individual beverages, because they were non-alcoholic. Temperance campaigners and 'teetotallers', from the children's Christian group the Band of Hope to the Salvation Army, were generous in their praise: tea was 'the cup that cheers but not inebriates'; coffee, likewise, was preferable to beer or gin. 'Coffee taverns' were even set up in the 1870s, in the hope of luring the poor away from the 'demon drink'.

Unfortunately, the coffee tavern had a gaudier and rather more appealing rival – the gin palace.

GIN PALACES AND PUBLIC HOUSES

But the gin-palaces are the lions of Drury-lane; they stand in conspicuous positions, at the corners and crossings of the various intersecting streets. They may be seen from afar, and are lighthouses… resplendent with plate glass and gilt cornices, and a variety of many-coloured inscriptions. One of the windows displays the portrait of the "NORFOLK GIANT," who acts as barman to this particular house; the walls of another establishment inform you, in green letters, that here they sell "THE ONLY REAL BRANDY IN LONDON," and a set of scarlet letters announces to the world, that in this house they sell "THE FAMOUS CORDIAL MEDICATED GIN, WHICH IS SO STRONGLY RECOMMENDED BY THE FACULTY." Cream Gin, Honey Gin, Sparkling Ale, Genuine Porter, and other words calculated utterly to confound a tee-totaller, are painted up in conspicuous characters, even so that they cover the door-posts.

MAX SCHLESINGER, *SAUNTERINGS IN LONDON*, 1853

Above: *Gin palaces could be rowdy places. Pubs served as off-licences, too – note the child taking a bottle home to the family; another child begs her father to come home.*

At the beginning of the nineteenth century, it was common for men of all classes to visit public houses. For the aristocracy, this was admittedly slumming and typically involved a visit to a 'sporting' establishment. This might include a respectable pub, such as the Coach and Horses on St Martin's Lane where the ex-boxer Ben Caunt, was landlord, or a seedier establishment with a reputation built around clandestine bouts of badger-baiting or cock-fighting. For the middle classes, pubs might be venues for public or charity dinners and other convivial get-togethers, typically held in pub meeting rooms, as well as for a quiet drink. For the lower classes, the pub was simply the place for relaxation and entertainment after a hard day's work.

As the century progressed, however, the pub fell out of favour with the middle classes, and was left to the poorer ranks of society. One reason for this was the success of the temperance movement, which suggested that drinking alcohol was respectable only if done in small doses at home. Another factor in the change of fortune of the public house was the rise of the gin palace.

The Glitz of Gin

Gin palaces flourished in the 1830s. They were brightly lit, ornately decorated rivals to the traditional public houses and the beer-shops created under the Beer Act of 1830, which stated that anyone could sell beer for a two-guinea licence. They not only sold gin, but also beer, such as pale ale and porter; the two could even be combined in a punch of warm ale and gin, known as 'purl'. Some would sell more expensive brandy and possibly some cordials. Whiskey, however, was not widely sold in London until the 1870s.

It was an article of faith with social commentators of the time that these gaudy

Above: A barmaid from Sketches of London Life, *1849. Note the Victorian beer pump and the pewter* tankards. *Opposite:* The Princess Louise in Holborn, *built in 1872 and refurbished in 1891, features ornate wall tiles and exquisite cut and gilt mirrors.*

enterprises were encouraging public drunkenness on an unprecedented scale. Whether they actually had such an effect is by no means certain. What these new drinking establishments did achieve, by doing away with traditional layout and practices, was to maximize sales and profit.

The traditional public house at the start of the nineteenth century was similar to a respectable private home, with the customers' space consisting of two rooms in the house – a tap-room, and, for the more genteel, a more comfortable parlour. The landlord, meanwhile, had an office area and private parlour – the bar and bar parlour. Drinks would be supplied by pot-boys, waiters or barmaids, who circulated between the bar, cellar and other rooms. It was only in the early 1800s that the concept of counter service was gradually introduced, with a small section of the bar opened up to allow customers to place an order

directly. The first gin palaces simply took this idea and ran with it – separate areas were done away with, and drink was served in a spacious single room over a long counter, behind which bottles and casks were proudly displayed. No space whatsoever was wasted on tables and chairs – customers drank standing up.

Another contrast between the older pub and the new gin palace, was that traditionally the pub had a bland, unprepossessing exterior, while the gin palace was brightly illuminated, gilded and signposted.

Thus, as these more commercial – and, allegedly, debauched – establishments began to replace public houses, there was something of an exodus of middle-class drinkers, who preferred a little more refinement.

A New Style of Pub

As it turned out, the gin palace of the 1830s, with its long counter and large open-plan space, was as much subject to the vagaries of fashion and demands of commerce as the old public house it competed against. By the early 1870s, typical gin palaces and public houses alike were increasingly being replaced by a new interior design, which fused elements of the two styles.

This new style of pub retained the old concept of separate areas for different classes of drinkers, but its drinking areas (the public and private bars) were more likely to be separated by decorative screens than walls. Moreover, they were served from a single long projecting central counter to which they each had partitioned access. This projecting counter, forming a promontory in the centre of the pub, made perfect business sense, maximizing the space available to serve customers.

Unlike older gin palaces, the new establishments also contained some seating, more in the manner of the traditional pub. The result was snug private bars, small areas where only a handful of people might sit and talk. These 'snugs' were particularly popular with groups of women as they allowed them to drink unmolested by men – public bars were still very much a male domain – and with those who wanted privacy for more illicit reasons. The snugs also allowed the landlord to charge a small premium for the privilege of privacy. By the 1890s, hinged 'snob screens' of metalwork or frosted glass were even placed about the counter in private bars, so that drinkers need not even see the bar staff.

Needless to say, temperance campaigners did not approve of the new style of pub any more than the old. Yet this did not inhibit a boom in the building of such establishments. And, unlike their predecessors, many of these later Victorian buildings have survived. True, in a great many cases, they are no longer pubs – Oxford Street, for instance, which once had nineteen drinking places, can now only boast one, the Tottenham, although most of the other pub buildings have not been actually demolished, but converted into shops. Nearby, the magnificent Horse Shoe, which was built in 1877 and adjoins the Dominion Theatre in Tottenham Court Road, now contains a mixture of cheap shops, restaurants and burger bars. Its façade is dirty and decaying, with no trace of its original use visible. Likewise, many suburban pubs have been converted into residential property.

Fortunately, however, there are still a few impressive Victorian pubs in London. Most notable are the Prince Alfred in Maida Vale (built 1863), which contains half a dozen bars divided by ornate mahogany and cut-glass screens, and the Princess Louise in Holborn, which was built in 1872 and refurbished in 1891. The Princess Louise's interior – all ornate gilt mirrors and tile-work – is striking, although its relatively uninteresting façade means it attracts few passers-by. Both are recommended to quench a thirst.

Below: The use of snob screens above bars, such as these in The Cock, off Oxford Street, which could be turned to block bar staff from view, was commonplace in the late Victorian period, providing a peculiar type of privacy.

FOOD FOR THE POOR, FOOD FOR THE RICH

A menu suggestion for the poor from a pamphlet issued by the London School Board in 1878:-

***Sheep's Head and Pluck.**–Thoroughly clean the head, put it into a saucepan with three pints of cold water, a cupful of rice, four onions sliced, and a little salt. Set it on a slow fire to cook very gently, skim it when it boils, and put in two carrots and two turnips cut in quarters. Let it simmer two hours. A quarter of an hour before serving, carefully skim off all the fat, and season to taste with a little pepper and salt. The liver may be fried, and the heart stuffed and baked, or both may be stewed together in one pint of water (after being browned in the saucepan with an ounce of dripping) for one hour, the gravy to be thickened with half an ounce of flour.*

***Below:** Baylis's cook-shop in Drury Lane specialized in feeding, lodging and providing help and advice to 'ticket-of-leave men' – prisoners on probation.*

A menu from the Holborn Restaurant in 1899:

SOUPS.
Purée of Hare aux croûtons.
Spaghetti.

FISH.
Suprême of Sole Joinville.
Plain Potatoes.
Darne de saumon. Rémoulade Sauce.

ENTRÉES.
Bouchées à l'Impératrice.
Sauté Potatoes.
Mutton Cutlets à la Reforme.

REMOVE.
Ribs of Beef and Horseradish.
Brussels Sprouts.

ROAST
Chicken and York Ham.
Chipped Potatoes.

SWEETS
Caroline Pudding.   St. Honoré Cake.
Kirsch Jelly.

ICE
Neapolitan.

CRIME AND PUNISHMENT

THEFT

Never enter into conversation with men who wish to show you the way, offer to sell "smuggled cigars" or invite you to take a glass of ale or play a game at skittles.

If in doubt about the direction of any street or building, inquire at a respectable shop or of the nearest policeman.

Do not relieve street-beggars, and avoid bye-ways and poor neighbourhoods after dark.

Carry no more money about you than is necessary for the day's expenses. Look after your watch and chain, and take care of your pockets at the entrance to theatres, exhibitions, churches, and in the omnibuses and the streets.

ROUTLEDGE'S *POPULAR* GUIDE TO LONDON, C. 1873

London has always had its share of con-men and pick-pockets, and nineteenth-century visitors to the capital were generally advised to protect their watch-chains, silk-hankerchiefs and purses from prying hands, especially at the theatre and in other crowded localities. Likewise, visitors to fairs and public places of entertainment were often cautioned by Victorian commentators about confidence tricksters, whose efforts to mystify gullible tourists could include anything from gambling games, such as the card trick 'Find the Knave', to mock auctions, where goods of dubious quality would be sold under false pretences.

It must have seemed to strangers reading such warnings that nowhere was safe. Indeed, even in the most fashionable parts of the metropolis, tourists were told to watch out for members of the 'Swell Mob' – smartly-attired pickpockets dressed as gentlemen, mingling unseen with their betters. But it is hard to say how much these perceived dangers reflected day-to-day reality.

Was Nowhere Safe?

Certainly, not every perpetrator of crime was a 'professional' criminal. A good proportion of petty theft was carried out by the poor and desperate, ragged men, women and children who stole food from shops or costermongers' barrows simply in order to eat or obtain a few pennies. Equally, of those who were professional thieves, for every skilled pickpocket, con-man and member of the Swell Mob, there were countless others who were simple oppor-

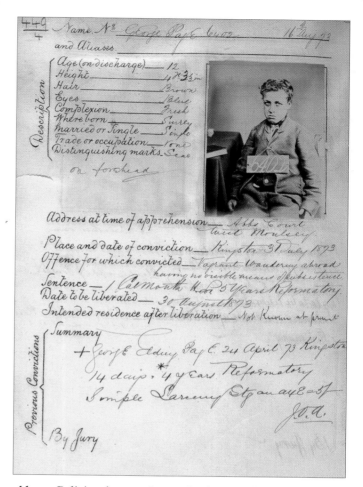

Above: Policing became increasingly systematic during the nineteenth century. Using photographs had obvious advantages, but Victorian criminologists also hoped they might discover a distinct criminal physiognomy.

Opposite: The Royal Courts of Justice, designed by G. E. Street, were opened by Queen Victoria on 4 December 1882.

tunists, including 'carriage-thieves' who stole from parked vehicles; 'lobby-sneaks' who stole items left in hotel or railway lobbies; and 'area-sneaks' who used the space outside the basement kitchens of London houses, known as the 'area', to break into homes.

Even in the case of burglaries, although skilled burglars with skeleton keys and lock-picks did exist, it was widely known that the best way to gain access to a home was by bribing a servant. Burglary, however, was a serious worry for the homeowner in London. For example, following a break-in, Jane Welsh Carlyle, wife of the essayist Thomas Carlyle, slept with a loaded pistol beside her bed during redecoration of her house in Chelsea, 'thieves having become aware of the state of the premises'.

THE DISCOVERY OF "JACK THE RIPPER'S" FIRST MURDER.

Above: Both cheap, racy fiction known as 'penny dreadfuls' and 'true-crime' stories, were popular among the urban poor.
Below: The gentleman's spiked collar was a satirical suggestion from Punch *for preventing 'garotting' – mugging by strangulation.*

The Romance of Crime

Trying to compare the level of crime in the nineteenth century with today is almost impossible. All we can say with certainty is that the Victorians were as fascinated by and fearful of crime as we are now. One obvious parallel is how much they enjoyed both crime fiction and 'true-crime' stories. Admittedly, the latter often had a serious message about reforming society, interweaving accounts of crime and criminals with social commentary. The best example of this type is James Greenwood's vivid *Seven Curses of London* (1869) – 'Neglected Children', 'Professional Thieves', 'Professional Beggars', 'Fallen Women', 'The Curse of Drunkenness', 'Betting Gamblers' and 'Waste of Charity'.

Fiction could fulfil a similar political purpose: one thinks of Charles Dickens' criticism of the Poor Law in *Oliver Twist* (1838), a book set in large part among the criminal underclass. But, for every *Oliver Twist*, there were many more 'penny dreadfuls', cheap and racy publications that sold in their thousands, chronicling the exploits of thieves and murderers; exploring the 'dens' and 'sinks' of the capital; explaining thieves' slang and glamourizing the criminal underworld for the purpose of entertainment. It was such publications and 'gallows literature' – supposed genuine confessions of executed criminals, including details of their crimes – that were blamed by social commentators and politicians for corrupting the minds of the nation's youth and turning them to crime, not unlike the way violent cinema, television or video games are often held responsible today.

VIOLENCE

The walk through the Dials after dark was an act none but a lunatic would have attempted, and the betting that he ever emerged with his shirt was 1,000 to 60. A swaggering ass named Corrigan, whose personal bravery was not assessed as highly by the public, once undertook for a wager to walk the entire length of Great Andrew Street at midnight, and if molested to annihilate his assailants.

The half-dozen doubters who awaited his advent in the Broadway were surprised about 1 a.m. to see him running as fast as he could put legs to the ground, with only the remnant of a shirt on him...

'ONE OF THE OLD BRIGADE', *LONDON IN THE SIXTIES*, 1908

We can concede, at least, that pickpocketing and thieving were an ever-present risk in the capital, especially where crowds gathered. Robbery with violence, on the other hand, was not so commonplace, though some areas of London were more notorious than others.

Unsafe Streets

Two of the most infamous districts were the slum of Seven Dials, near Covent Garden, and the Ratcliff Highway in the East End, a beery haunt of brawling sailors and drunken prostitutes. Both were notoriously dangerous places for travellers, especially after nightfall. Along the Ratcliff Highway were dozens of pubs, cheap dance halls, freak shows, and low-rent theatrical entertainments, all geared towards relieving seafarers of their money while on shore. Rowdy nights on the town often ended with fist fights between men of different nationalities or from different ships, and stabbings often settled an argument.

It was a brave 'gentleman' who entered such a low district without the support of the police. The police, however, were generally happy to act as paid guides to interested parties. Charles Dickens made several such trips, investigating how the police operated in the capital; his article 'On Duty with Inspector Field', for instance, famously records one journey to the notorious 'Rat's Castle' area of St Giles.

Yet, for all their notoriety, heightened by the accounts of Dickens and lesser writers, Seven Dials and the Ratcliff Highway were the exception rather than the rule. Indeed, the stereotyped image of Victorian London as a grim fog-ridden place, haunted by thieves and murderers, conjured up by films featuring Dr Jekyll and Mr Hyde or Jack the Ripper, is misleading. Street-lighting by gas, and then electricity, made the nocturnal streets of the capital increasingly safe as the century progressed, and the new police force, which was founded by Sir Robert Peel in 1829, was a highly visible symbol of authority that improved the security of travellers immensely.

Serious Crime

There were occasional panics: the 1850s and 1860s saw public anxiety reach fever pitch about 'garotting': the mugging of pedestrians by strangulation. In

Above: *Seven Dials was a notoriously violent slum. The monument at its centre today is a recreation of the Sundial Pillar that stood at the intersection of the seven roads that gave the district its name.*

1862, the Member of Parliament Hugh Pilkington was attacked in such a fashion on the way to his club in Pall Mall. The resulting press hysteria led to a rash of severe sentences being handed out by judges, and a backlash against what was seen as the mild treatment of convicts, especially the ticket-of-leave (parole) system. Yet, there were only ever a handful of genuine garotting incidents; and the intense reaction to such crimes was, if anything, symptomatic of their rarity and shock value.

Likewise, the awful Jack the Ripper murders of the 1880s, which still loom so large in our collective memory, struck fear into Londoners precisely because nothing so shocking had happened in the capital during Victoria's reign. In fact, to make a comparison, the Victorians had to think back to the Marr and Williamson murders of 1811, in which two entire families were killed in their homes on the Ratcliff Highway within twelve days of each other. And, although the Ripper case led to a good deal of anxiety and made people more wary of walking alone at night, it also attracted the morbid excitement that still surrounds it today. It was not long before wealthy West-enders were getting together to tour Whitechapel and the crime scenes.

Above: This Punch *cartoon of two rain-soaked prostitutes has the one asking the other, 'How long have you been gay?' – 'gay' was Victorian slang for prostitution.*

VICE

Going to the Opera, I met in the Strand one Sarah Tanner, who in 1854 or 5 was a maid of all work to a tradesman in Oxford Street: a lively honest rosyfaced girl, virtuous & self-possessed. A year or so after, I met her in Regent St. arrayed in gorgeous apparel. How is this? said I. Why, she had got tired of service, wanted to see life and be independent; & so she had become a prostitute, of her own accord & without being seduced. She saw no harm in it: enjoyed it very much, thought it might raise her & perhaps be profitable. She had taken it up as a profession, & that with much energy: she had read books, and was taking lessons in writing and other accomplishments, in order to fit herself to be a companion of gentlemen. And her manners were improved—she was no longer vulgar...

ARTHUR MUNBY, *DIARY*, 1859

The most visible criminal elements on Victorian streets were not thieves, con-men, or, needless to say, murderers, but prostitutes. For a minority, prostitution was an informed, discreet personal choice, weighing up the pros and cons of the sex industry against that of the drudgery of 'service'. Indeed, if one could hook up with a gentleman of means, then a life of comparative luxury beckoned as a 'kept woman'. A handful of such women even went on to marry into the aristocracy. But, of course, these were the exceptions.

A Sordid Necessity

For most, prostitution was a sordid necessity, generally to supplement a meagre income. Many prostitutes worked by day as needle-women or in some other poorly-paid industry, and sold their bodies when money ran low. Prostitution was rarely a glamorous calling. It is often forgotten, for instance, that four out of five of Jack the Ripper's prostitute victims were in their forties, and had each given birth to several children. These were not coquettish demi-mondaines (to use an elegant Victorian term), but simply desperate women, living hand-to-mouth in slum lodgings, on the fringe of Victorian society.

Much of the trade of prostitutes was conducted in London's back streets, like those in Whitechapel, or in cheap lodgings and rooms let by the hour. Some lodging-houses were, in fact, brothels by any other name. There was even, supposedly, a class of prostitutes known as 'dress-lodgers', who not only rented rooms but gaudy clothing from their landlord. While walking the streets, they would, we are told, be followed by an old woman, who kept an eye on the landlord's investment – in case they absconded with the dress.

Prostitution was not confined to the East End or the slums, however. A far more infamous vice district for most of the century was the Haymarket, described by one writer in 1857 as 'a cancer in the great heart of the Metropolis'. Today, the area is devoted to tourists, theatres and restaurants. To the Victorians, however, the district was synonymous with vice.

Above: Despite the grandeur of John Nash's Theatre Royal, the Haymarket was a notorious haunt of prostitutes.

Indeed, if visiting the Haymarket Theatre or Opera House, it was necessary for a paterfamilias to shepherd his wife and daughter to the very doors of the building, in case they encountered the area's nocturnal denizens.

The Brothel Business

In large part, the problem was the 'night-houses' and 'supper-rooms' of the Haymarket, which were essentially late-night clubs for well-to-do young men whose hobbies were drinking, gambling and whoring. Kate Hamilton's was the most renowned of these resorts, and the eponymous proprietress reputedly 'weighed at least twenty stone, and had as hideous a physiognomy as any weather-beaten Deal pilot'. Other well-known night-houses included Mott's, The Kitchen and Jack Percival's. None were brothels per se, but they attracted young men from the upper classes who were out for a good time and women who were either professional prostitutes or actresses, ballet-girls and such like, who were considered to have loose morals, and thus to be little better.

Moreover, regardless of the supper-room crowd, the Haymarket itself, like nearby Regent Street, was simply a well-known meeting ground for prostitutes and clients. There you would find all levels of women of the night, from ragged flower-girls for whom

Above: A policeman interrupts proceedings in an upmarket brothel patronized by the upper classes. These were often known euphemistically as 'Introducing Houses'.

Above: Robert Peel, Prime Minister 1834–5 and 1841–6, founded the Metropolitan Police in 1829; hence police constables became known as 'bobbies' or 'peelers'.

selling flowers was not necessarily the principal trade, to well-dressed women with furnished private rooms in adjoining streets. Some of the flower-girls were actually children. Indeed, it was only in 1875 that the legal age of consent was raised from twelve to thirteen years, and then to sixteen years in 1885, which perhaps gives an idea of the age of many of the girls involved in the trade.

Another district associated with vice, suprising to anyone who knows modern London, was the Strand, and, in particular, Holywell Street, a narrow thoroughfare immediately north of the two churches of St Clement's Danes and St Mary-le-Strand. Rather than prostitution, however, Holywell Street was famous for its bookshops, and, in particular, the sale of 'low publications' – often quite graphic pornography – which were shown or advertised in the street's shop windows, attracting crowds of onlookers. This profitable trade was reduced somewhat by the passing of the Obscene Publications Act in 1857, and a series of police raids, but persisted until the street itself was demolished in the Kingsway/Aldwych development of 1900–1905.

The thieves, con-men, garotters and 'fallen women' all had, of course, a common enemy – the policeman.

POLICING THE METROPOLIS

The London policeman is the stranger's friend. If you are in search of an acquaintance and only know the street where he lives, apply to the policeman on duty in that street, and he will show you the house, or at least assist you in your search. If you lose your way, turn to the first policeman you meet; he will take charge of you and direct you. If you would ride in an omnibus without being familiar with the goings and comings of those four-wheeled planets, speak to a policeman, and he will keep you by his side until the "bus" you want comes within hailing distance. If you should happen to have an amicable dispute with a cabman—and what stranger can escape that infliction?—you may confidently appeal to the arbitration of a policeman. If, in the course of your peregrinations, you come to a steam-boat wharf or a railway-station, or a theatre or some other public institution, and if you are at a loss how to proceed, pray pour your sorrows into the sympathetic ear of the policeman.

MAX SCHLESINGER, *SAUNTERINGS IN AND ABOUT LONDON*, 1853

Above: Bow Street Magistrates Court was built in 1879–81. The Magistrates, or Police, Court dealt with lesser criminal offences; serious cases were heard at the Old Bailey.

Above: An 1895 engraving from The Graphic *showing a scene from the rough East End; the caption read: 'A policeman's lot is not a happy one'.*

The Metropolitan Police Force was founded by Sir Robert Peel in 1829, so 'bobbies' or 'peelers' were a common presence on the streets by the start of Victoria's reign eight years later. Before Peel's efforts, the policing of the capital had been left to parish constables and night-watchmen, popularly known as 'Charlies'. However, as the metropolis grew, it was clear that a new co-ordinated force was needed, not least because the parish constable or watchman rarely followed wrong-doers outside the confines of his own parish.

A Unified Force

By 1839 the Metropolitan Police had amalgamated all pre-existing London 'forces' – including the Bow Street Runners, which had been founded in the 1740s by Henry Fielding, and the Marine Police, which was founded in 1798 to prevent pilfering from ships and dockyards. In fact, the only hindrance to creating a London-wide institution was the City of London, which insisted on its own separate force; founded in 1839, it remains a separate body to this day.

And yet, in the 1830s, despite widespread contempt for the old system – the 'Charlies' were infamously sluggish and incompetent – many Londoners loathed the new force. Its members were mocked as 'Blue Devils' and policemen were regularly seriously assaulted. In particular, there were fears that the new force impinged on personal liberty and was a step towards a 'police state'.

Fortunately, its professional organization and competence eventually won over many doubters. The police were carefully subdivided into divisions, each of which had a hierarchy of Superintendent,

Above: The Metropolitan Police relocated to New Scotland Yard, designed by architect Norman Shaw, in 1890. The Portland stone used in the building was quarried, rather appropriately, by Dartmouth convicts.

Inspectors, Sergeants and Constables. Constables were given regular beats to patrol and 'fixed points' at which they were stationed at night. A standard blue uniform and hat were issued and helmets were introduced in the mid-1860s; each policeman displayed a unique identification letter and number on his collar; and truncheons were designated as the policeman's principal weapon – fears had existed that cutlasses would be used. Everything was done to create a 'professional' force and thereby allay public concern.

Moreover, in 1842, a separate Detective Department (albeit containing only two Inspectors and six sergeants) was also formed, to tackle more complex or important cases. The detective branch was based in the Scotland Yard offices of the Police Commissioners who ran the force. The name of Scotland Yard – an inoffensive courtyard in Whitehall, which the police offices happened to overlook – has denoted the Metropolitan Police's headquarters ever since, even though the offices have moved twice: in 1890 to new buildings on the Embankment, and in 1967 to St James's.

PUNISHMENT

COURT: Have you any witnesses to speak to your character, boy?

BOY: Yes, my Lord; fifteen gen'lm'n is a vaten outside, and vos a vaten all day yesterday, vich they told me the night afore my trial vos a comin' on.

COURT: Inquire for these witnesses.

Here, a stout beadle runs out, and vociferates for the witnesses at the very top of his voice; for you hear his cry grow fainter and fainter as he descends the steps into the court-yard below. After an absence of five minutes, he returns, very warm and hoarse, and informs the Court of what it knew perfectly well before – namely, that there are no such witnesses in attendance… the boy is sentenced, perhaps, to seven years' transportation. Finding it impossible to excite compassion, he gives vent to his feelings in an imprecation bearing reference to the eyes of 'old big vig!' and as he declines to take the trouble of walking from the dock, is forthwith carried out…

CHARLES DICKENS, *SKETCHES BY BOZ*, 1836

If the police caught a criminal, then the next step was the courts, whether the humble Police Court (the equivalent of the modern Magistrates' Court) for a minor offence, or the Old Bailey, also known as the Central Criminal Court, for more serious charges. The rules of the courts were somewhat different from those of today; for example, in Old Bailey cases, an accused was not allowed to give evidence under oath, lest he perjure himself; this was the case until 1898.

Transportation

Punishment could come in forms we now consider unacceptable. This included not only capital and corporal punishment, but also transportation to Australia. The sentence of transportation was, more-over, often passed for what we might now consider a relatively minor offence, such as pick-pocketing. The six-month journey, followed by exhausting physical labour, was not an easy option. It was, however, preferable to the death penalty, which had been apllied only a few decades earlier under the remnants

Above: The treadmill, seen here above the exercise yard in Coldbath Fields Prison (closed 1880s), was a pointless, physically exhausting punishment, involving 'walking' on steps attached to a revolving drum just to keep it moving.

of the 'Bloody Code' of the previous century, when capital punishment was considered suitable for some two hundred offences. Transportation continued until 1868, by which time Australia had become more prosperous and many were actually paying to emigrate there.

The Prison System

Throughout Victoria's reign, the punishment for most criminals was, of course, neither transportation nor death but imprisonment. This was never a pleas-ant experience but, in the first half of the century, treatment within prisons varied widely, according to type of prisoner, whim of the governor and the local authority under which it was managed. Debtors' prisons, such as the Marshalsea (in which Charles

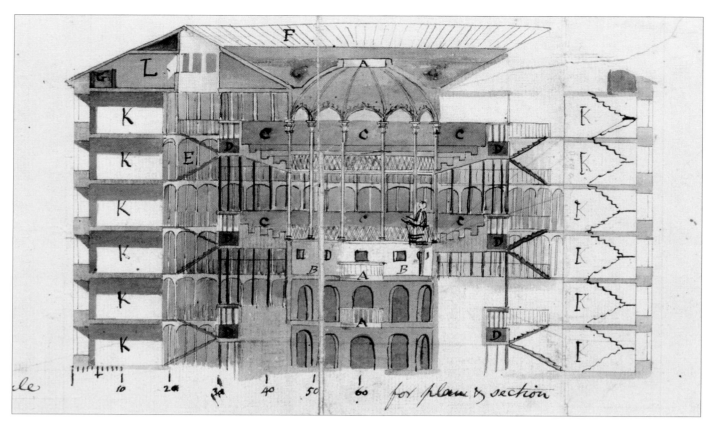

Above: The Panopticon was Utilitarian philosopher Jeremy Bentham's (1748–1832) plan for a model prison. It was designed to allow maximum surveillance of all prisoners.

Dickens's father was incarcerated) and The Queen's Bench, were notoriously lax in their arrangements, with prisoners allowed many personal luxuries and daily visits from relatives and friends.

Other prisons, on the other hand, went to the opposite extreme. Pentonville, for instance, was opened in 1842 as a 'model' prison, and incorporated the latest in design. Cell-blocks radiated from a central hub, in accordance with the 'panopticon' style, so that, theoretically, warders were able to view prisoners in different areas from the central point. The prison was also run along the lines of the latest thinking in prison management: the 'separate system'. The system's principal tenet, as outlined in a House of Lords report of 1835, was that keeping prisoners separate from each other was 'necessary for preventing Contamination, and for securing a proper System of Prison Discipline'. In Pentonville, this meant not only entirely separate cells, but separate cubicles for each prisoner in the prison chapel, face masks whenever they gathered together and identification by a given number rather than by name.

Talking to other prisoners was strictly forbidden and entailed further punishment. Unsurprisingly, with such total isolation, Pentonville became famous for its high rate of suicide and mental illness.

The 1860s and 1870s brought in more government regulation. Debtors' prisons became redundant when individuals were given the right to declare themselves bankrupt. Moreover, by 1877, all London prisons were under the control of the Home Office, rather than individual local authorities. However, increasing centralization and standardization did not mean an easier life for those at Pentonville and elsewhere, rather often it meant the opposite. In fact, in 1865 the Assistant Director of Prisons, Sir Edmund du Cane brought in a regime of 'Hard Bed, Hard Board, Hard Labour', designed to make prisons across the country as consistently unpalatable as possible.

Hard Labour

If prison living had once appealed to a small minority – it was reputed, for instance, that the homeless would occasionally break a window or commit some minor vandalism to get a few nights of warmth and food – du Cane's reforms probably had the desired effect. Hammocks were replaced by planks, food was made deliberately tasteless and monotonous, the

Above: Wormwood Scrubs, a prison planned by Sir Edmund du Cane and built by convict labour between 1874 and 1890, operated under the 'separate system'.

'silent system' was introduced (talk was forbidden) and, worst of all, repetitive, highly strenuous but pointless physical labour was made an obligatory part of prison routine. These tasks included picking oakum (separating strands from old rope, for recycling), the dreaded treadmill (a large rotating drum with steps, which prisoners walked on to keep it moving) and the crank (a handle which prisoners had to rotate a given number of times). Discipline and regimentation was the watchword. It was only as the century progressed that some questioned this approach, and more useful jobs began to take place – but the treadmill was only finally banned in 1898.

Many Victorian prison buildings are still used for their original purpose, including Pentonville, Wandsworth and Wormwood Scrubs. They are not, however, in marvellous condition, and in December 2000 the Director of the Prison Service suggested they all be sold for real estate development and the profits reinvested in new jails outside the capital; it seems, however, that his suggestion has not been taken up.

EXECUTION

I was a witness of the execution at Horsemonger Lane this morning. I went there with the intention of observing the crowd gathered to behold it, and I had excellent opportunities of doing so, at intervals all through the night, and continuously from day-break until after the spectacle was over... I believe that a sight so inconceivably awful as the wickedness and levity of the immense crowd collected at that execution this morning could be imagined by no man, and could be presented in no heathen land under the sun. The horrors of the gibbet and of the crime which brought the wretched murderers to it faded in my mind before the atrocious bearing, looks, and language of the assembled spectators.

CHARLES DICKENS, 'LETTER TO THE EDITOR OF *THE TIMES*', 13 NOVEMBER, 1849

At the start of the Victorian era, public hangings in London generally took place outside Newgate Prison, which was demolished in 1902 and replaced by the present Old Bailey, or outside Horsemonger Lane Gaol in the Borough, which was demolished in 1880.

Above: When the bells of St Sepulchre's chimed eight o'clock it was the signal for the hangings to commence outside Newgate prison. Thousands of onlookers would fill the cross-roads in front of the church to watch the grisly spectacle.
Below: In this Punch *cartoon of 1849, entitled 'The Great Moral Lesson', a jolly crowd awaits a hanging outside Horse-monger Lane Gaol, while children play in the background.*

A Common Spectacle

Public hangings had the air of a Bank Holiday – crowds would gather as early as the previous evening, with gin shops and public houses opening throughout the night and street-hawkers keeping the ever-increasing mob supplied with pies or cakes. Poor members of the populace, if sufficiently agile, would climb lampposts for the best view, while the wealthy hired houses, shop windows and rooftops, perhaps bringing a hamper of food to sustain themselves. By the morning of the hanging, the area surrounding the place of execution would be impassable due to sheer numbers of people.

Newgate hangings were generally at eight o'clock on a Monday morning, with the bells of the nearby church, St Sepulchre's, heralding the start of the proceedings. The condemned man or woman was brought out from Newgate Prison onto the temporary scaffolding, a few words would be spoken by the Newgate Ordinary (chaplain), a hood was placed over the prisoner's head and the trap-door was opened by the hangman William Calcraft, who held the post from 1829 to 1874. Far from maintaining a respectful silence, the crowd generally erupted into cheering when the execution was over. There was a good trade in souvenirs and printed stories of the murderer's final 'confession', which was frequently an invention of the publisher.

The writers William Thackeray and Charles Dickens both attended and reported on hangings in the 1840s, and were appalled by the spectacles they saw. The satirical journal *Punch*, likewise, inveighed against the jovial nature of the crowds, who were often drunk and certainly did not seem to draw the 'Great Moral Lesson' that the advocates of the death penalty believed in. Twenty years later, the authorities were persuaded to move hangings to inside the prison walls. The last man to be hanged in public in England was Michael Barrett in 1868, a Fenian who had set off explosives outside a Clerkenwell jail in a desperate attempt to rescue two of his comrades.

NOTORIOUS LONDON CRIMINALS

1840
François Benjamin Courvoisier
A Swiss valet who slit the throat of his elderly employer, Lord Russell on the night of 5 May 1840, following a petty disagreement. He was hanged at Newgate on 6 July 1840. The fact that Courvoisier was a foreigner and his employer was a peer of the realm caused the murder to attract a great deal of attention.

1849
Mr and Mrs Manning
This conniving couple killed Patrick O'Connor, a customs officer, after inviting him to dinner in Bermondsey on 9 August 1849. Having shot him with a pistol and finished him off with a crowbar, they buried him in a grave they had already pre-pared beneath their paved kitchen floor. The motive was predominantly robbery, but the case had a frisson of sexual intrigue as O'Connor was Maria Manning's former suitor, and they had been having an affair. Mr and Mrs Manning were hanged at Horsemonger Lane Gaol on 13 November 1849, watched by a crowd of thousands.

The Mannings murder combined all elements of notoriety: sex, money and violence.

1864
Franz Muller
A German tailor who bludgeoned Thomas Briggs, an elderly bank clerk, for his gold watch on the evening of 9 July 1864. The unusual feature of the case was that the murder took place in a railway carriage on the North London railway. The seats of the carriage were drenched with blood and the body was thrown onto the tracks. Muller fled to New York, but was captured. He was hanged at Newgate on 14 November 1864.

1870
Margaret Waters
Margaret Waters was hanged at Horsemonger Lane Gaol on 11 October 1870 for the murder of an infant in her care. Waters was a 'baby-farmer' who took in and, supposedly, cared for young children for a fee, no questions asked. Baby-farmers were notorious for their deliberate neglect. They had little to gain from properly tending to their charges, as most of the children were illegitimate, and the baby-farmer often received just a single lump sum as payment for their services.

1872
William Chester Minor
This former US Army officer shot dead a brewery worker in Lambeth in the early hours of 17 February 1872. The case was dubbed 'The Lambeth Tragedy'. Minor was found to be mentally ill and committed to Broadmoor. There he became a volunteer lexicographer for the *Oxford English Dictionary*.

1874
Arthur Orton
Orton made his name as the 'Tichborne Claimant'. A Wapping-born butcher living in Sydney, Australia, Orton returned to England in 1866 claiming to be Roger Tichborne, the heir to a baronetcy and large estates who had been lost at sea in 1854. Orton gained the support of Roger's mother, who was obsessed with finding her son. Legal proceed-ings taken by Orton in 1871 failed and he was charged with perjury. He was sentenced on 28 February 1874 to fourteen years penal servitude. Released in 1884, Orton died in poverty four years later.

1888
Jack the Ripper
Between 31 August and 9 November 1888, a serial killer murdered five women in Whitechapel, east London. Countless theories still circulate about other possible vic-tims and the identity of the attacker. 'Jack the Ripper' was a *nom de guerre* used by a letter-writer who claimed responsi-bility for the crimes. His letter was published by the police in the hope that his handwriting might be recognized.

1892
Thomas Neil Cream
A convicted back-street abortionist and poisoner, Cream was given clemency and released from an American prison in 1891. He relocated to England and settled in Lambeth where he committed a fresh series of poisonings, killing several young women. Bizarrely, he drew attention to himself by accusing his neighbour of the crimes and by attempting to blackmail the man's family. He was hanged on 15 November 1892, allegedly claiming, at the moment of his execution, to be Jack the Ripper, despite the fact he was in prison in Illinois throughout 1888.

CEMETERIES

CHURCHYARDS, BURIAL GROUNDS AND VAULTS

Grannie was buried in the vaults of St. Martin's Church, Trafalgar Square, her coffin being laid upon that of Uncle Hugh. The vaults were a very awful place – coffins piled upon one another up to the ceiling, and often in a very bad state of preservation – and the funeral was a very ghastly one, all the ladies being enveloped in huge black-hooded mantles, which covered them from head to foot like pillars of crape.

AUGUSTUS HARE, *THE STORY OF MY LIFE*, 1896

The writer Augustus Hare was born into a wealthy family in 1834, and attended his grandmother's funeral at the age of fourteen. Unfortunately, despite its size and architectural splendour, St Martin's-in-the-Fields, like most of the churches in central London, was profoundly ill-equipped to cope with requests for interments, even from the best families. For, by the 1840s, most of London's ancient churchyards, vaults and burial grounds had long since been filled up by previous generations of Londoners.

Overcrowding Underground

Overcrowding was a long-standing problem, exacerbated by the city's growing population. By the mid-nineteenth century, it was not uncommon, where the situation was at its worst, for multiple unrelated bodies to be buried in one grave. Dr Hector Gavin, investigating public health in the poor district of Bethnal Green in 1848, was told that the limit was 'as many [bodies] as can be packed in 15ft deep… sometimes twelve [bodies]'. In some cases, Gavin found that the ground had even been raised up to cover the numerous bodies interred. Likewise, there was an infamous case in the 1840s where the owner of a chapel near Fleet Street was found to have 'interred' 12,000 bodies in its vaults – an impossible figure. It came to light that the corpses were being surreptitiously removed and dumped on a regular basis.

And it was not simply a question of inadequate space: the old churchyards were becoming a serious health hazard, with rotting corpses frequently exposed by grave-diggers attempting to squeeze in another coffin. Charles Dickens famously described one such plot in *Bleak House* (1851), a place 'pestiferous and obscene, whence malignant diseases are communicated to the bodies of our dear brothers and sisters who have not departed', and, though writing fiction, he was not exaggerating. Dr John Simon, commissioned by the City of London to report on public health, had bluntly stated two years earlier, 'every dead body buried within our walls receives its accommodation at the expense of the living'.

Opposite: This Corinthian temple, topped by four angels, is one of the more dramatic memorials at Kensal Green Cemetery; it marks the grave of Mary Gibson (1854–72).
Below: Medieval churches, such as St Olave's on Hart Street, could not provide enough burial space for London's growing population. Dickens nicknamed this particular churchyard 'St Ghastly Grim', for the stone skulls above its gates.

Above: 'Mutes', silent attendants paid to walk in funeral processions, were a feature of middle-class Victorian burials.

Dr Simon's principal concern was the ever-present threat of communicable disease, not least cholera, which reached epidemic levels in 1831–2 and 1848–9, and was the contagion most feared by the Victorians. It was commonly believed that the disease was carried by 'miasma' (noxious smell), and so the stinking churchyards seemed a very real threat to public health.

Clearly something had to be done. In fact, an attempt to address the problem had been made some twenty years earlier.

CEMETERY COMPANIES

'Such affectionate regret, sir, I never saw. There is no limitation, there is positively NO limitation:' opening his eyes wide, and standing on tiptoe: 'in point of expense! I have orders, sir, to put on my whole establishment of mutes; and mutes come very dear, Mr Pecksniff; not to mention their drink. To provide silver-plated handles of the very best description, ornamented with angels' heads from the most expensive dies. To be perfectly profuse in feathers. In short, sir, to turn out something absolutely gorgeous.'

CHARLES DICKENS, *MARTIN CHUZZLEWIT*, 1844

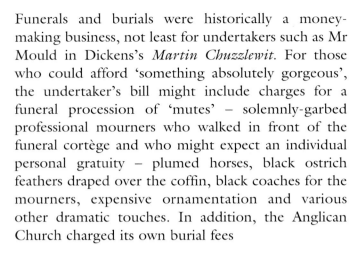

Funerals and burials were historically a money-making business, not least for undertakers such as Mr Mould in Dickens's *Martin Chuzzlewit*. For those who could afford 'something absolutely gorgeous', the undertaker's bill might include charges for a funeral procession of 'mutes' – solemnly-garbed professional mourners who walked in front of the funeral cortège and who might expect an individual personal gratuity – plumed horses, black ostrich feathers draped over the coffin, black coaches for the mourners, expensive ornamentation and various other dramatic touches. In addition, the Anglican Church charged its own burial fees

Undertaking Innovation

In the 1820s, however, the barrister George Frederick Carden (1798–1874) saw a gap in the market. He began to promote a novel business venture, which he hoped might serve a dual purpose: to make a profit – for those willing to invest their money – and to alleviate the overcrowding of London's ancient churchyards. He proposed to revolutionize the business of burial entirely, by importing an innovation that had already proved successful on the continent and which was finding favour elsewhere in the country – the cemetery.

It may seem odd to modern readers, but the cemetery – a planned place for interments not adjoining the local parish church – was a rather revolutionary concept. True, there were a handful of separate small 'burial grounds' already in the capital, but these were exceptions. The best known was Bunhill Fields, off the City Road. This particular ground was never consecrated, and so became the favoured resting place of 'Dissenters' – Methodists, Baptists, Congregationalists, Wesleyans, Quakers et al. – who objected to interment in ground owned and blessed by the Anglican Church. Consequently, it ended up housing several famous names, including leading nonconformist John Bunyan (1628–88), novelist Daniel Defoe (1660–1731), hymn-writer and poet Isaac Watts (1674–1748) and painter and poet William Blake (1757–1827). But Bunhill Fields was a mere five-acre plot that had been enclosed and used for burials since the seventeenth century; full to capacity, the last interment took place here in 1854. Carden's proposals in the 1820s were on a much grander scale.

For Carden's inspiration was not English, but French – Père Lachaise in Paris to be exact, the first

great cemetery in Europe to resemble a grand landscaped garden. It is now the resting place of a diverse set of individuals, including composer Frédéric Chopin (1810–49), novelist Marcel Proust (1871–1922), dramatist and poet Oscar Wilde (1854–1900) and rock singer Jim Morrison (1943–71). To Carden, Père Lachaise seemed ultra-modern, visually attractive and presented a disease-free alternative to the foul churchyards of London.

The General Cemetery Company
After several years spent acquiring backers and petitioning the government, a General Cemetery Company was finally formed in 1832. Shares were issued and 54 acres of land were purchased in Kensal Green, on the north-west edge of the city. In part, it

Above: Bunhill Fields was one of only a handful of burial grounds in London at the start of Victoria's reign, as most burials were in local parish churchyards.

was the cholera epidemic of 1831–2 that persuaded parliament of the value of this new hygienic burial place; and in part, it was the result of almost a decade of campaigning by Carden and others.

The first burial took place in the General Cemetery of All Souls, Kensal Green, in 1833. The new business proved remarkably successful, and by 1840 the Company's share price had doubled. The success of Kensal Green spurred on various imitators and within a decade a total of seven large suburban cemeteries had been constructed across London and its outskirts.

Above: *Abney Park Cemetery opened in 1840. Its grounds, which were once a neatly cultivated arboretum, declined in the twentieth century.*

Opposite: *The bizarre Graeco-Egyptian tomb of circus proprietor and performer Andrew Ducrow (1793–1842) in Kensal Green Cemetery, where Greek, Gothic and Egyptian designs stand side by side.*

DESIGN

> *Let us now speak of the institutions of Highgate: the most modern is the cemetery, which was consecrated by the Lord Bishop of London in May, 1839, and has therefore the merit of being one of the first, as it is undoubtedly one of the most beautiful in situation… It contains about twenty acres of ground on the side of the hill facing the metropolis. The approach to it through Swain's Lane conducts the visitor by a green lane rising gradually to the Gothic building which forms the entrance. Entering the grounds, the eye is struck by the taste everywhere displayed. Broad gravel paths on either side wind up the steep slope to the handsome new church of St. Michael's, which is seen to great advantage from almost every part of the grounds. An hour may be very well spent here musing on the dead.*

> J. EWING RITCHIE, *ABOUT LONDON,* 1860

What were the new cemeteries like? For a start, it should be noted that the 'joint-stock company' cemeteries were not created for the common good of

Londoners, but principally to make a profit for investors. Tower Hamlets, with its East End location, ended up largely a poor man's cemetery, and by 1851, eighty per cent of its burials were in public graves – common plots for the poor who had made no provision for a private burial. However, this was the exception. The remainder of the 'big seven' hoped to acquire a more middle-class clientèle – and the money that came with them. This aspiration was reflected in how the cemeteries were designed, with features that would appeal to prospective clients.

A Garden of Rest

One aspect that all the companies considered was the physical environment, which is hardly surprising given the cramped and noxious state of many urban churchyards. Firstly, the cemeteries were landscaped and then planted with trees and shrubs, in order to present a scenic aspect to anyone walking the grounds. Indeed, it is important to remember that the overgrown ivy-clad sites we see today are not what the Victorians intended – the original cemeteries were much more like parks. Kensal Green's layout, in particular, was consciously modelled on John Nash's Regent's Park, with a circular walk at its centre. Likewise, Abney Park's grounds, formerly those of a local mansion, were a famous arboretum, with its trees and shrubs conscientiously labelled with their names for the education of visitors.

Secondly, the new cemeteries were also made to appear as imposing and secure as possible. The practice of 'body-snatching' – robbing graves of corpses to sell to anatomists for dissection – was only tackled by the Anatomy Act in 1832, which allowed unclaimed bodies of the poor to be utilized by the medical profession. Even after this date, it was not unknown for bodies in the packed City churchyards to be exposed accidentally by grave-diggers or animals. Therefore, there was a commercial advantage in providing a resting place that presented high walls and substantial gates, as were constructed at Kensal Green. Many of the companies also offered places in secure underground catacombs, which were perceived as more exclusive than a simple grave or tomb.

Open to All

In addition to the creation of an appealing physical environment, the cemetery companies also ensured that there were fewer of the restrictions and regulations associated with churchyard burials. Most importantly, some provision was made for the 'Dissenters' and 'nonconformers' who did not want any connection with the Anglican Church. Abney Park, in fact, was not consecrated at all, and a third of its burials were of nonconformists; the other cemeteries followed the example of Kensal Green and either had (or, in the case of Brompton, planned to build) separate Anglican and Dissenters' Chapels, and kept separate burial areas for the two groups. Kensal Green also set the tone by not laying down any rigid rules for the style of monuments – resulting in a strange mixture of Egyptian, Greek and Gothic mausolea.

All these features were innovations; and they made the new cemeteries appealing to both investors and clients. So much so, in fact, that in the early 1850s an even grander plan was drawn up – Brookwood Cemetery, which is perhaps the most remarkable of these ventures, if only for its sheer ambition.

The Final Journey

Brookwood was founded in 1852, when 'The London Necropolis and National Mausoleum Company' bought 2,000 acres of land in Woking, Surrey, 400 acres of which were prepared and laid out in the modern style.

When the new cemetery finally opened, in November 1854, it was the largest in the world, many times the size of its seven commercial competitors in London, which only covered between 30 and 60 acres each. Moreover, Brookwood, situated in the Surrey countryside, was twenty miles further away from the metropolis than any of the 'big seven', which meant burial plots could be cheaper. The only obvious impediment was, of course, this very distance. If the cemetery was intended to serve central and southern London, how would people get there?

Top left: The Molyneux family tomb at Kensal Green Cemetery, which originally boasted a church-like spire, is a fine example of the Victorian Gothic style.

Left: The entrance to the Necropolis Railway Station, which once took both the deceased and mourners to Brookwood Cemetery in Surrey, is at 121 Westminster Bridge Road.

RESTING PLACES OF FAMOUS VICTORIANS

KENSAL GREEN
Harrow Road, W10
Opened 1833
Thomas Hood (1799–1845)
Poet.
Sir Marc Isambard Brunel
(1769–1849) Engineer, dug the first
tunnel under the River Thames.
Isambard Kingdom Brunel
(1806–59)
Engineer.
William Makepeace Thackeray
(1811–63)
Novelist.
Charles Babbage
(1791–1871)
Mathematician, inventor of machine computing.

Isambard Kingdom Brunel

Anthony Trollope (1815–82)
Novelist.
Wilkie Collins (1824–89)
Novelist.
Charles Blondin (1824–97)
Tightrope walker.

WEST NORWOOD
Norwood Road, SE24
Opened 1837
Thomas Cubitt (1788–1855)
London property developer.
Mrs Isabella Beeton (1836–65)
Cookery writer.
Charles Spurgeon (1834–92)
Famous preacher and founder of the
'Metropolitan Tabernacle'.

HIGHGATE
Swain's Lane, N6
Opened 1839
Pierce Egan (1772–1849)
Writer and dramatist.
Michael Faraday (1791–1867)
Physicist and chemist.
George Eliot (1819–80)
Novelist.
Karl Marx (1818–83)
Political philosopher and economist.
Christina Rossetti (1830–94)
Poet.
John Galsworthy (1867–1933)
Novelist and dramatist.
Radclyffe Hall (1880–1943)
Novelist and poet.

NUNHEAD
Linden Grove,
SE4
Opened 1840
Sir Wallis Budge
(1856–1934)
Egyptologist.

Michael Faraday

ABNEY PARK
Stoke Newington High Street, N16
Opened 1840
James Braidwood (1800–1861)
London's fire chief, killed on duty.
William Booth (1829–1912)
Religious leader and founder of the
Salvation Army.

BROMPTON
Fulham Road, SW10
Opened 1840
Sir Samuel Cunard (1787–1865)
Shipping magnate.
George Godwin (1815–88)
Architect and editor of *The Builder*.
Emmeline Pankhurst (1858–1928)
Suffragette.

A remarkable and typically Victorian solution was found: bodies, together with mourners, were conveyed to the cemetery by special train. 'Coffin tickets' were issued, and there was the usual division of travellers into first, second and third class. Better still, a dedicated 'Necropolis station' was built near Waterloo, and locomotives travelled daily to the cemetery, which, within its grounds, had not only two separate chapels for Anglican and Dissenters, but two separate railway stations, North and South.

Today, it all sounds a little bizarre, yet Brookwood met with initial success. The company was, however, somewhat over-ambitious in its original purchase of 2,000 acres and, within a few years of opening, was obliged to sell some of its land. The train service, moreover, became less regular in the twentieth century, ceasing entirely after the Necropolis station was bombed during the Second World War.

Brookwood, however, still operates on a commercial basis as a local cemetery.

PUBLIC CEMETERIES

'A friend gave me half a sovereign to bury my child. The parish provided me with a coffin, and it cost me about 3s. besides. We didn't have her taken away from here not as a parish funeral exactly. I agreed that if he would fetch it, and let it stand in an open place that he has got there near his shop until the Saturday, which was the time, I would give the undertaker 3s. to let a man come with a pall to throw over the coffin, so that it should not be seen exactly that it was a parish funeral.'

HENRY MAYHEW (REPORTING WORDS OF THE WIFE OF A DOCK LABOURER) IN A 'LETTER TO THE *MORNING CHRONICLE*', 1849

The rash of commercial cemeteries inaugurated by Kensal Green in 1833 ended with Brookwood in 1854. By the late 1840s, it was becoming clear that, although the new cemeteries were popular with the middle classes, they were not the answer to over-crowding in the capital. The bad conditions persisted in London's old churchyards, vaults and burial grounds. For the commercial companies did not cater for many of the poor, who frequently ended up in old crowded common graves. While the joint-stock companies pointed the way, something different was needed.

Health Issues

The poor simply could not afford decent funerals and burials. Yet there was a strong desire to show some public token of respect for deceased relatives, and this itself could have harmful side effects. It was not uncommon, for instance, for a body to be left decomposing for several days in somebody's home, generally in an open coffin, while money was begged and borrowed to pay the requisite funeral costs. Even in those cases where payments had been made during the deceased's lifetime to a 'burial club' in order to provide for funeral arrangements, there was often no perceived urgency. Thus, with no understanding of hygiene and how disease might spread, slow or lax

Above: *The poor often saved up for burials in order to avoid the shame of a parish funeral.*

funeral arrangements encouraged the spread of disease, especially in confined urban tenements.

When a cholera epidemic struck London in 1848–9, there was suddenly a strong impetus to tackle sanitation problems, including the issue of burial. Parliament's response to an earlier epidemic of the same disease in 1832 had been to support the creation of Kensal Green Cemetery. In 1848, however, a new approach was tried – namely, the Government itself stepped in. A public body was created, the 'General Board of Health', which had responsibility for creating new cemeteries, for forbidding burials in specific church-yards (if required) and for purchasing the commercial cemeteries and putting them under state control.

The Parish Cemetery

The General Board of Health, however, actually achieved very little, due to various political constraints imposed upon it, only managing to purchase one of the commercial cemeteries – Brompton. Nonetheless, a precedent was set, and in 1852 the Metropolitan Burial Act was passed, allowing public money to be spent by local parishes on the construction of new cemeteries. Parish 'Burial Boards' were to take responsibility for 'receiving houses' to hold corpses, the administration of burial fees and numerous other issues.

The ancient burial grounds and vaults in central London were closed and the initial flourishing of the commercial cemeteries was over. The first publicly owned cemetery was built in 1854 by the St Pancras Burial Board in Finchley, which was then a rural area several miles north of the city. Other parishes swiftly followed this example.

Naturally, the owners of the joint-stock cemetery companies were somewhat worried. However, Kensal Green and its successors did not decline immediately after the parish cemeteries appeared; rather, their popularity and competitive edge slowly diminished over decades, and several would only gradually fall into disuse and disrepair during the twentieth century.

Decline and Decay

It is difficult to pick out one single causal factor in the decline of the cemeteries. Certainly, the many parish cemeteries provided substantial subsidized competition. In some cases, the cemetery companies themselves suffered from mismanagement and fraud. Cremation also grew in popularity, once the Cremation Society was founded in 1874. And, come the twentieth century, people came to disdain what was perceived as the pomp and excess of Victorian monuments and funeral customs.

Above: *One of the many stone angels that grace the gravestones in Abney Park Cemetery, Stoke Newington.*

Above: *Abney Park's chapel has fallen victim to vandalism and decay, as have those in other commercial cemeteries.*

Indeed, the whole business of the Victorian funeral – the mutes with their hats garlanded in black crape, women buying fresh mourning dresses for every death, black jet jewellery and black-bordered stationery – all seemed rather morbid and indulgent. Likewise, the monuments – angels, broken columns (symbolizing the death of the head, or the 'pillar', of a family), inverted torches (representing the extinguished life), funerary urns and grand mausolea in the shape of Greek temples – came to be seen as ostentatious or inappropriate.

Fundamentally, however, London's commercial cemeteries had the same problem that afflicted their predecessors: they simply filled up. Moreover, maintenance costs increased, the economic climate changed and they were no longer a money-making proposition.

By the 1970s several of the 'big seven' had fallen into virtual disuse, the original companies were bankrupt and the cemeteries themselves were overgrown and dangerous, with graves invaded by spreading vegetation. All were subject to routine vandalism, and monuments were defaced and destroyed with depressing regularity. Abney Park's chapel, for instance, was gutted by arson; only its rather ghostly shell remains, and many of the old company's records were lost in the fire.

Fortunately, today, things are much improved for the likes of Highgate, Abney Park and Nunhead. Managed by a combination of local councils and charitable bodies of 'Friends' devoted to their preservation, they are increasingly seen as valuable conservation areas, 'urban jungles' for insect and bird life, and provide unique venues for leisure and educational activities.

HEALTH

SANITARY RAMBLINGS

PARADISE-ROW… These houses present all the external characters of decency and comfort; nevertheless, the following fact will explain how much the health of the inhabitants is dependent on external circumstances:- A gentleman, named Knight, rashly, and in ignorance of the locality, purchased the lease of No. 1, which forms the eastern end of Bethnal-green-road. Immediately after taking up his residence there he became ill, and, shortly after, died of typhus, in an aggravated form. On inspection of the neighbouring premises, I discovered Paradise Dairy immediately behind his house. In this dairy sixteen cows and twenty swine are usually kept. The animal remains and decomposing vegetable refuse were piled up a considerable height… Moreover, the soakage from the neighbouring privies found its way into this receptacle for manure and filth.

HECTOR GAVIN, *SANITARY RAMBLINGS*, 1848

Improvements in arrangements for burial did do a great deal to improve the health of the Victorian metropolis. The changes made in the 1850s were, however, symptomatic of a wider concern about public health. Indeed, from the 1840s onwards, the Victorians became increasingly interested in such issues, and, in particular, the living conditions of the poor. One reason for this heightened interest was that the lives of the worst-off were being documented in books and newspapers by a number of 'social investigators', who were determined to provoke debate and stimulate change.

Poverty Bred Disease

Hector Gavin, a doctor and lecturer in medicine based at Charing Cross Hospital, was one such individual. In the 1840s he made enquiries into the day-to-day lives of the urban poor. He focused upon the relationship between living conditions, lack of basic sanitation and disease. In two books, *The Unhealthiness of London* (1847) and *Sanitary Ramblings* (1848), he offered his support to a theory that, though radical, was growing in popularity. Namely, that the poverty and disease ubiquitous in the slums of London were not simply the symptoms of moral failings among the poor, but the result of the overcrowded and insanitary conditions in which they were forced to live. Poverty bred disease, and disease, in turn, bred poverty, by leaving men unfit for work.

To modern readers it may well seem odd that this was debatable. Nonetheless, there were some who held to the belief that the poor brought suffering upon themselves, through laziness or vice. To suggest, therefore, that conditions in the slums could be improved primarily by changing environmental, rather than moral factors, was a radical approach.

Opposite: The National Hospital for Neurology in Queen's Square was originally a charitable foundation that opened in 1860, although the present building dates from 1885.

Below: A cross-section of typically unhygienic 'low lodgings'. Note the large numbers of men crowded into the small rooms and the open sewer running directly beneath the building.

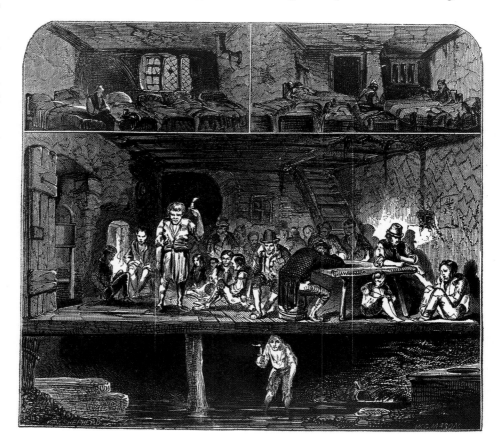

The Workhouse

The most prominent proponent of this position in the 1840s was, however, not a doctor or a journalist, but Edwin Chadwick, architect of the New Poor Law of 1834, and secretary to the Poor Law Commissioners. Chadwick was an unpopular but energetic bureaucrat who had become convinced that the Poor Law, which he himself had helped to frame, was not functioning as well as he had hoped. This was the infamous legislation that created Union workhouses, prison-like institutions for providing food and shelter for the destitute, which were operated under strict regimes, deliberately offering minimal support and sustenance, amounting to less than any inmate might obtain as a labourer.

The workhouses were, in part at least, designed as a deterrent to anyone who might attempt to take

excessive advantage of handouts from their local parish. But, for this deterrent to operate effectively, applicants had, at least, to be fit to work in the first place. Chadwick, having investigated the practical operation of the Poor Law, particularly after a typhus epidemic in London in 1837–8, which noticeably increased numbers applying for 'relief', concluded that the new system failed to address one of the root causes of over-reliance on the state – disease.

It was not merely that sick men and women could not be made to work, and would often end up in the workhouse; this was, perhaps, inevitable. Rather, what struck Chadwick was statistical evidence, published in the new medical journals, such as *The Lancet*, which showed widely different rates of mortality across the country. By the 1840s, it was becoming clear that life

Above: The reformer Edwin Chadwick (1800–1890) was an unpopular bureaucrat, yet he was instrumental in lobbying for improved sanitation for the poor.

Below: Westminster Union Workhouse was where the parishes of Westminster could admit their paupers for local 'relief' – basic food and lodging in return for manual labour.

expectancy varied between town and country, between one city and another, sometimes between different areas within a city and, most strikingly, between different social classes.

Chadwick's own research, not least his ground-breaking report entitled *Sanitary Conditions of the Labouring Population*, which was published in 1842, suggested that issues such as water supply, ventilation and air quality were important factors in explaining these differences. It therefore followed that there was something practical that could be done to address the problem: improving living conditions and, in particular, tackling defects in drainage and sewers. Such actions would reduce disease among the poor, and thus reduce 'pecuniary burdens' on the state and boost the economy. Edwin Chadwick, therefore, devoted his energies to lobbying for change.

Contagions

Not everyone adopted Chadwick's utilitarian approach. Other sanitary reformers appealed to the self-interest of the middle and upper classes, by stressing the ever-present danger of zymotic (infectious) diseases in the capital, not least the spread of cholera, which was particularly dreaded. Indeed, it was clear to most Londoners that contagions that began in the unhealthy slums swiftly spread into respectable districts, and did not respect social rank or moral virtue. Others, of a more evangelical bent, suggested that the lower classes would never be susceptible to improving influences without first obtaining decent living conditions. As Charles Dickens, in a speech to the Metropolitan Sanitary Association in 1850, put it: 'sanitary reforms must precede all other social remedies... neither education nor religion can do anything useful until the way has been paved for their ministrations by cleanliness and decency.' Fortunately, whatever their reasons, many rallied behind Chadwick's appeal for sanitary improvements.

Cholera, of course, was not the only potentially fatal contagion in the Victorian metropolis; typhus, typhoid, tuberculosis, smallpox, influenza and pneumonia all claimed thousands of lives in London in the 1840s. Cholera was, however, a new illness, which had slowly spread from Asia to England, via Eastern Europe, in the early 1830s. Death from cholera was

Above: This cartoon by Robert Cruikshank (1789–1856) shows a cholera patient experimenting with various ineffective remedies.

shocking and spectacular: it could kill within a day, with intense vomiting and diarrhoea which left the body with shrunken features and terribly dehydrated, often resulting in a bluish tinge to the skin.

Thus, it is unsurprising that cholera was especially feared – there was, moreover no hope of a cure; between forty and sixty per cent of those infected survived the disease, but survival seemed to be in the lap of the gods. Medicine in this period had no certain cure for any contagious disease, although the possibility of vaccination against smallpox had been discovered in the 1790s and was made compulsory for infants in 1853.

Cleanliness is Next to Godliness

In the mid-nineteenth century, therefore, at the time Hector Gavin was writing his book, the only hope was

Above: Campden Baths and Wash-houses in Hampstead operated from 1888 until 1978, providing cheap public baths and laundry facilities to promote cleanliness among the poor.

Below: Baths for both rich and poor were dotted throughout the capital. The more luxurious offered a range of unusual spa treatments, including bathing in 'magnetic' water.

prevention. Personal hygiene was not ignored: even with an imperfect understanding of how diseases were spread, most Victorians believed that clean clothes and bodies were advisable. Some even considered that washing had physical and spiritual benefits beyond mere cleanliness; as *The Pictorial Handbook of London* (1854) put it: 'It is Christian, and it is politic in a worldly sense; it is a beginning towards the salvation of soul and body, by cleansing the body and purifying the mind'. Consequently, a parliamentary act of 1846 encouraged local authorities to build public baths and wash-houses for the poor, in which they could pay a couple of pennies for hot or cold baths, and women could do their laundry in decent conditions.

Edwin Chadwick and his supporters, however, were interested in change on a grander scale and, in 1848, it seemed like his lobbying was having an effect, when a new raft of public health measures were finally passed by the government.

MIASMA

Whenever a house smells close and fusty to a person coming in out of the open air, it is always unhealthy, and sooner or later will produce illness in those who live in it. The good health that persons who live in houses in open country places enjoy is entirely owing to the pure air they breathe. But even in country villages the air is often rendered unwholesome by cesspools or dung-heaps being kept close to the house, or by the filthy habit of throwing the house-slops and dirty water on the ground close to the door.

W.B. Tegetmeier, *The Scholar's Handbook of Household Management and Cookery*, 1876

Chadwick's campaigning was rewarded, in the midst of a cholera epidemic, by the 1848 Public Health Act and the Nuisances and Diseases Prevention Act. The legislation created a national 'General Board of Health' and gave the option for local authorities throughout the country to create local Boards of Health and employ 'Medical Officers'. These officers would, in turn, make enquiries into the spread of infectious disease, and report back to local authorities with suggestions for improvements.

Sewer Squabbles

The capital itself was to be served by a Metropolitan Commission of Sewers, whose members would include Chadwick and many of his supporters. Moreover, the act obliged new houses to be constructed with connections to public sewers, where sewers were available, and to include either a water-closet or privy. It must have seemed, despite the ravages of cholera throughout the metropolis, as if a great leap forward had finally been made by the reformers. Here, after all, was an organization that could co-ordinate efforts to remove 'nuisances' – dung-heaps, over-flowing cesspools, waste from factories and slaughterhouses – and develop proper drainage and sewerage throughout the city.

It soon emerged, however, that there were problems, which were largely political in nature. There was genuine resentment at the intrusion of central government, which the General Board of Health represented. Many contended that all sanitary reform was an undue infringement of personal liberty, that such matters were solely concerns for the individual and

Above: *Constructing an effective sewerage system for London was a mammoth task.*

private business. Commentators were also suspicious of the 'policing' role of the Medical Officers, with one article in *The Times* comparing Chadwick to a military dictator, in his supposedly ruthless aggregation of powers unto himself and the new public bodies.

There was also a good deal of dissent from a wide range of vested interests, including local landlords,

Above: 'Father Thames Introducing his Offspring to the Fair City: Diphtheria, Scrofula, Cholera.' In 1858 the 'Great Stink' made sewerage a high piority. **Below:** Sir Joseph Bazalgette (1819–91), designer of London's sewers and the Thames Embankment, caricatured as a sewer-serpent.

vestries (local parish authorities), the innumerable local 'paving boards' responsible for the maintenance of roads and, not least, the existing water companies who were loath to change their business practices. To top it all, it was not long before commissioners were engaged in acrimonious debate over the appropriate design for a new system of sewers.

A Lack of Medical Knowledge

An additional difficulty faced by Chadwick and his supporters, though they did not realize it themselves, was a fundamental lack of understanding about the nature of the diseases they faced, and how they were transmitted. Chadwick was a staunch believer in the theory, popular for much of the century, that disease was principally caused by foul smell, or 'miasma'. He, therefore, ignored the possibility that cholera and typhoid were transmitted in polluted water, and recommended flushing sewers directly into the Thames. Most of London's water supply for drinking and bathing was drawn from the river, so water carrying cholera was recycled again and again throughout the city. Fascinatingly, even when a London doctor, John Snow, mapped cholera cases in Soho in 1854, demonstrating that they centred round a pump drawing water from an infected well, with cases falling away once the pump was removed, the 'miasmatists' were still not convinced – the idea was firmly entrenched.

As it turned out, Edwin Chadwick did not hold onto his position as Commissioner of Sewers, not least because of heated quarrels with his colleagues, and he rapidly lost political influence. The commission itself, sitting in various incarnations from 1848 until 1854, also seemed increasingly ineffectual, as it discovered it had insufficient funds and powers to carry out the schemes it planned. It was finally replaced in 1855 by the Metropolitan Board of Works, whose members were to be elected by local vestry authorities. This gave each of the various districts of the metropolis an individual voice on how the sewer schemes would develop, thus countering any concerns about 'Chadwickian' tyranny.

The Metropolitan Board of Works was the body that would revolutionize public health in London.

THE GREAT STINK

For years past the deterioration of the river has been noticed; and from time to time endeavours have been made to direct attention to the subject as one of great public interest. Every day increases the evil. Without taking into consideration the immense annual growth of London, it must be borne in mind that other large districts give their refuse to the river. There are also gas-works, most unwholesome manufactories, slaughter-houses, cow-sheds, stables, breweries, and the drainage of thickly-filled graveyards, to aid the mischief; and yet intelligent men can be found to maintain the salubrity of the Thames. The health of thousands must be affected by it, and what may occur cannot be calmly contemplated.

GEORGE GODWIN, *TOWN SWAMPS AND SOCIAL BRIDGES*, 1859

Above: The Victorians were justifiably proud of their engineering feats, and functional buildings, such as the pumping station at Abbey Mills, Stratford were incredibly ornate.

The Commissioners of Sewers were seen as ineffectual by contemporary critics, but they had set a precedent for central regulation of sewers and sanitation, and, if nothing else, arranged for detailed maps of London's sewers and drains to be drawn up by the government's Ordnance Survey department, an essential precursor to any programme of building. They had also employed the services of a certain engineer, Joseph Bazalgette, who, in 1856, went on to work for the Metropolitan Board of Works.

Bazalgette's Labyrinth

Bazalgette was well-qualified for the job. Apart from his experience with the Commissioners, he had testimonials from eminent men such as Isambard Kingdom Brunel and Robert Stephenson. Within six months, he presented a plan that drew on ideas that had already been put forward to the defunct

Commission of Sewers. The plan detailed a system of intercepting sewers running west to east (three to the north of the river, two to the south), which would link up with the existing networks and carry all London's sewage away from the centre of the metropolis. The system would cost the remarkable sum of over £2 million, involve the construction of over eighty miles of underground tunnels, and the creation of pumping stations in east London that would raise sewage to a height from which it could continue its journey to outfalls at Beckton and Crossness.

It was a vast and ambitious scheme, but many believed it was essential. Unfortunately, it was subject to further wrangling over the location of the outfalls, which Sir Benjamin Hall, representing the government, considered were still within the limits of the metropolis, albeit its sparsely populated hinterlands. Thus, he argued, Bazalgette's proposal contravened the legal remit of the Board, which had been to make 'sewer and works for preventing all or any part of the sewage of the Metropolis from flowing or passing into the Thames in or near the Metropolis'. Fruitless debate on the matter continued until mid-1858 when matters came to a head as a result of a natural phenomenon – 'The Great Stink', the popular name given by the press to the stench that emanated from the Thames in the hot summer of that year.

The Stinking Thames

The Thames, of course, had never been particularly fragrant. It was a convenient dumping ground for all sorts of industrial and municipal waste, including residues from dozens of riverside factories. But the summer of 1858 was different, both due to weather conditions and, ironically, the impact of slightly improved sanitation. For it was the increasing use of water-closets in private households, connected to the existing sewers (rather than waste being emptied into a cesspit and collected by 'night soil men') that was flushing more and more human waste into the old drains, all of which eventually led into the Thames.

Moreover, as a tidal river, the filth was not immediately washed away, but was carried back and forth by the tide. For the many Londoners who

Right: The engine room of the sewage pumping station at Crossness, east London, which was completed in 1865, has been lovingly restored to its original grandeur.

Above: The Victoria Embankment was built between 1864 and 1870 to conceal the new sewers and tunnels; it replaced a ragged riverbank with a spacious boulevard.

believed in the danger of miasma, the very smell of the river was life-threatening. In the newly built Palace of Westminster, which abutted the river, Members of Parliament were said to be overcome by the fumes. They hastened to grant the Metropolitan Board of Works full powers, and Bazalgette's much-delayed scheme was finally under way.

Considering the size of the scheme, it progressed with amazing speed. Much of the new sewer system was in operation by the mid-1860s, with the ornately designed pumping stations in east London, at Crossness and Abbey Mills, opening in 1865 and 1868 respectively. The Thames embankment, between Westminster and Blackfriars – an impressive achievement, which concealed not only the new sewers, but tunnels for the underground railway, plus gas and water pipes – was completed in 1870.

Throughout the work, Bazalgette proved himself a first-rate project manager, conducting regular tests on the quality of materials used by his builders. In consequence, amazingly, London still relies on Bazalgette's sewers.

As Bazalgette's plans came to fruition, the health benefits of the scheme were also made starkly obvious by a cholera epidemic in the summer of 1866. Just as it was cholera that stimulated concern about sanitation, it was this epidemic that proved the reformers were right. In 1866 the vast majority of cases occurred in the East End, among those supplied by the East London Water Company, which was not yet connected to the new sewers. Many who had previously doubted the disease could be water-borne were now convinced; the microbes responsible would actually finally be identified in the 1880s. Indeed, following the 1866 outbreak, there were no further epidemics of cholera or typhoid in the capital.

However, without diminishing the great importance of Bazalgette's improvements, he did not, and could not, solve all the health problems of the Great Metropolis.

ENGLISH MALADIES

In this moist climate of ours, and with the murky atmosphere of coal smoke which obscures the sunlight, where, in addition, thousands of tall chimneys vomit forth their impurities, how can it be otherwise than that the child, from want of exercise in fresh air, gets out of health and condition? The bones are imperfectly developed being soft and spongy they

bend beneath the body weight, nor can they resist the muscular contractions. How few families in London of even the better class escape wholly what is called rickets — 'the English malady', as the French call it.

JAMES CANTLIE, *DEGENERATION AMONGST LONDONERS*, 1885

'Degeneration' was a popular concept at the end of the nineteenth century. Essentially, the theory of degeneration was the reverse of Darwin's theory of evolution – that people might degenerate into an increasingly inferior breed of humanity. Dr James Cantlie found proof for this idea in the 'puny and ill-developed race' he observed in London. City life, he concluded, was robbing Londoners of exercise, ozone – which he believed was a critical ingredient for health – and sunlight. He was particularly struck by the pale skin of dwellers in the metropolis, compared to the healthy tanned complexions he saw in the countryside.

Living and Working Conditions

It is, of course, easy nowadays to find fault with Cantlie's ideas, not least his conviction about the healthiness of tanned skin and ozone, but his observations concerning the poor health of Londoners were real enough. The vitamin-deficiency disease of rickets was commonplace in the smog-bound capital, not only due to lack of sunlight, but to a poor understanding of nutrition. Malnutrition, arising from ignorance and poverty, was common among the lower classes. Minor deformities caused by rickets were taken for granted among both the rich and poor.

Not only did the poor often eat badly and live in dreadful conditions, they often worked in them as well: industrial illnesses particular to individual occupations were accepted as inevitable. The most famous example was the condition of 'phossy jaw'; this eroded the jaw bones of those involved in the production of phosporus matches, notably at Bryant and May's factory in Bow, where the condition was brought to public attention by the social campaigner Annie Besant in the 1880s. Many others also worked with hazardous materials and dangerous equipment, with little or no protection.

Finally, reforms relating to drainage and sewers, successful though they were, could do nothing about potentially fatal airborne infections, such as influenza and tuberculosis. There could be little doubt that the metropolis was a hostile environment.

Children, in fact, were at most risk. Indeed, worries about degeneration came to a head after the 1870 Education Act was passed and children were obliged to attend school. The physical condition of the poorest children became clearly visible to teachers. In the 1890s, in the worst districts one in six infants died before their first birthday.

Above: Sir James Cantlie (1851–1926), President of the Royal Society of Tropical Medicine and Hygiene, believed London's unhealthy air fostered physical degeneration.

Right: The Bryant and May Match Factory in Bow, east London, was infamous for its workers ravaged by 'phossy jaw' – bone erosion caused by contact with phosphorus.

Above: St Charles Hospital, Ladbroke Grove, was built in 1881 as a model workhouse infirmary for St Marylebone parish. Residents here were fortunate as workhouse provision for the sick was often primitive.

However, amid the disease and ignorance, there were many men and women who worked to improve matters. In particular, charities, hospitals, asylums and refuges all provided a degree of support for the poor and, as the century progressed, medical science made numerous advances.

HOSPITALS

LONDON HOSPITAL, WHITECHAPEL ROAD. Instituted 1740, incorporated 1759, for the relief of diseased and hurt manufacturers, seamen in the merchant service, labourers, women, children, and others. A yearly subscription of 5 guineas constitutes an annual governor, and a benefaction of 30 guineas a life governor. Every governor is *entitled to recommend one in-patient and four out-patients at a time. Subscribers of sums not less than 1 guinea annually may send out-patients.*

PETER CUNNINGHAM, *HAND-BOOK OF LONDON, 1850*

The hospital was not a Victorian invention, but the nineteenth century certainly saw a great many developments in London's health care system. Modern Britons, of course, are used to the National Health Service, which was founded in 1948 and where treatment for most ailments is available for free. The Victorians had an entirely different arrangement, which, especially at the start of Queen Victoria's reign, depended a good deal on one's position in society.

Medical Care for the Poor

In short, the well-off, including middle-classes families, if they could afford it, paid doctors for medical care, which they expected to receive in their own homes; this could even include operations. The working classes, on the other hand, were dependent on hospital care, provided by institutions run as charitable concerns, with money coming from endowments or, more commonly, charity fund-raising. These were known as 'voluntary' hospitals, as they were paid for by voluntary contributions; but, though charities, they were not made available to everyone.

Most did not admit children, people with obscure or infectious diseases or those with chronic ailments. Many hospitals also distinguished between the 'deserving' and 'undeserving' poor, in that treatment was only given to those who were respectable and likely to return to some form of employment. If the destitute and the long-term unemployed fell sick they could only hope for basic medical aid in grim workhouse infirmaries. Charles Dickens wrote of the wards in Wapping Workhouse in 1861, though admitting they were kept clean, 'They ought not to exist; no person of common decency and humanity can see them and doubt it'.

This system left many Londoners in difficulty if faced with serious illness. Those with communicable or other diseases not catered for in voluntary hospitals had few places to turn. In fact, until the 1860s, the Fever Hospital in Islington and two workhouse infirmaries were the only institutions taking infectious cases in the whole of London. Fortunately, the situation was gradually remedied as the century progressed by the appearance of an increasing number of specialist hospitals. These dealt with particular areas of the body or particular diseases; examples in the capital included hospitals for fistulas, cancer, smallpox and consumption.

Specialization

Specialization itself was, admittedly, not a new idea. 'Lying-in' (maternity) and children's hospitals had been founded in the metropolis in the eighteenth century, but the nineteenth century saw a rapid increase in numbers of specialist institutions.

Some were the result of government intervention, following the creation of a Metropolitan Asylums Board in 1867. This board was responsible for setting up a network of fever hospitals and separate workhouse infirmaries, served by special ambulances, to contain and isolate those with infectious diseases. Other specialist institutions were pet projects of charitable individuals. Others were, undoubtedly, the result of speculation by ambitious medical men, keen to earn themselves a remunerative reputation as a 'specialist' in the swiftest way possible. Nonetheless, all served a valuable purpose, and, though some complained that specialists lacked general doctoring skills, the new hospitals fostered high levels of expertise among their staff.

The rise of specialist hospitals did not, however, make medical treatment available to all; it still helped to have money. Of course, the poor had their free workhouse infirmaries, however badly run they might be. Yet, technically at least, these were only available

Above: A hospital ward in the Royal Free Hospital in Gray's Inn Road in 1895; this institution offered free medical care to those who could not afford treatment.

Right: In the nineteenth century, the Bethelehem Hospital (Bedlam) housed its lunatics in a Lambeth building, which is now home to the Imperial War Museum.

to the destitute and not the working poor. This restriction was only lifted in 1883.

There were also charitable dispensaries, which offered drugs and advice on an outpatient basis. However, they were not found in every district and some required paying subscriptions.

Even in 'voluntary' hospitals admission was never straightforward, as the income of these institutions was usually based on subscriptions from donors, and most followed the old custom of allowing their larger donors to become hospital governors and, in turn, to nominate cases for admission. This power was an incentive to donate, in that it allowed the governor to get preferential treatment for his servants and dependants. The practice eventually died out, but not until the second half of the century, and it was responsible for many deserving cases not receiving hospital care.

Interestingly, the middle classes faced an entirely different financial problem: many of them were too well-off and too proud to be admitted to charity hospitals, but too poor to afford a doctor at home. It was only in the 1880s, when large London hospitals like St Thomas's and Guy's began to accept some paying patients to boost their finances, that an alternative became available.

QUALIFICATIONS

BACHELOR OF MEDICINE
FIRST EXAMINATION, 1841
MEDICINE

1. You hare called to a fellow-student taken suddenly ill. You find him lying on his back in the fender; his eyes open, his pulse full, and his breathing stertorous. His mind appears hysterically wandering, prompting various windmill like motions of his arms, and an accompanying lyrical intimation that he, and certain imaginary friends, have no intention of going home until the appearance of day-break. State the probable disease and also what pathological change would be likely to be effected by putting his head under the cock of the cistern.

PUNCH, 1841

Punch's report of the award of the first medical degrees by the newly formed University of London, which was founded in 1836, suggests that the satirical journal did not have a high opinion of the sobriety of medical students. Nonetheless, the nineteenth century saw the image of medical practitioners change, from frequently being derided as 'quacks' to becoming respected professionals.

Doctors and Nurses

In particular, doctors were keen to be seen as 'gentlemen', and it therefore became increasingly desirable to obtain a full university education and medical school training if one wanted to practise medicine. To the same end, new or reformed professional and regulatory bodies were created. The transition of the College of Surgeons to the Royal College of Surgeons in 1843, for instance, included the introduction of examinations into the elections of Fellows of the Society. The British Medical

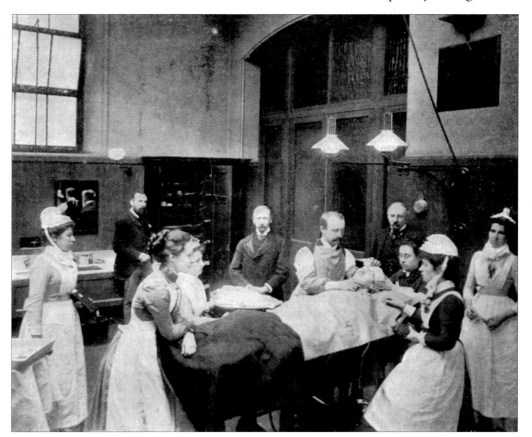

Association was formed in 1855, having grown from a provincial society founded in Worcester in 1816. Finally, in 1858, the General Medical Council was established by law, with the power to create a single register of qualified practitioners.

There were, of course, other people working in medicine, and the role of the nurse also grew in respectability during the nineteenth century, not least due to the efforts of Florence Nightingale (1820–1910). Nightingale first came to prominence by treating troops in the Crimean War (1854–7), acquiring the romantic title of the 'Lady of the Lamp' for her tireless attention to the wounded, day and night. Following the war, she returned to London and, among numerous other works, wrote *Notes on Hospitals* (1859), advocating improvements to ventilation, drainage and hygiene. The book proved immensely influential and, although Nightingale was a staunch miasmatist, new hospitals designed under the 'pavilion' plan (entirely separate well-ventilated wards) were nonetheless conspicuously successful in reducing the spread of infectious disease between patients.

Three of the large pavilion blocks of St Thomas's Hospital, constructed opposite the Houses of Parliament and opened in 1871, still survive today. It was also at St Thomas's that money provided by the

public, donated in Nightingale's honour, helped found the Nightingale Training School for nurses, which did much to raise nurses' status within hospitals, and, through the work of its alumni, helped introduce higher standards of patient care.

Above: *Queen Adelaide's Dispensary in Bethnal Green, east London, was built in 1865–6 and converted into flats in the 1990s.*

Right: *Florence Nightingale (1820–1910) became a national heroine for her work with soldiers in the Crimean War. She devoted her life to improving public health, and her writings on hospital design promoted hygienic conditions.*

Opposite: *Doctors and nurses undertake an operation in the operating theatre of the Royal Free Hospital, London, in 1895.*

There was, however, no obligation for nurses to be registered in the same way as doctors under the 1858 Medical Act until 1919. This was, in part, because many Victorian commentators (Florence Nightingale included) considered this detracted from the traditional 'vocational' aspect of the profession. Debates about the pros and cons of state regulation were, in fact, nothing new. The 1858 Medical Act itself, which established the General Medical Council and its register, though a landmark in regulation, was considered an intrusion by some and inadequate by others, since it did not prevent anyone offering medical services, as long as they did not represent themselves as a qualified doctors. In short, it did nothing to hinder the quacks.

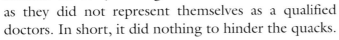

Above: 'Street doctors' made their money selling quack remedies to those who could not afford decent medical advice.

QUACKERY

Far from being in a position to record the extinction of the race of 'herbalists' and 'doctors for the million' who practise upon the poor, my investigations prove they are still about as numerous as their trade is lucrative.

THOMSON AND SMITH, *STREET LIFE IN LONDON*, 1877

Quackery was found in various forms in Victorian London. In an 1877 photographic study of London's poor, John Thomson – a pioneering photographer – and Adolphe Smith – a radical social journalist – found that 'pills, potions, and quack nostrums' were regularly sold on the streets. This was despite increased access to free hospitals and a growing number of clubs and friendly societies that offered health insurance schemes, where the poor paid small amounts each week into a common fund (which, in

turn, paid for a doctor). One street-seller assured Smith that a 'Blood Purifier', principally composed of sassafras, burnt sugar and water, was guaranteed to be lucrative, adding knowingly, 'If it don't lengthen the life of the buyer it lengthens the life of the seller'.

Lotions and Potions

Extravagant claims that formed part of the 'patter' of pedlars were not, however, exclusive to those who preyed on the poor. Adverts in newspapers, journals and books were aimed at the middle classes and regularly made promises that they could not possibly keep. 'Dr. Locock's Pulmonic Wafers', for instance, offered to cure not only coughs but asthma, consumption and influenza.

Others traded not in pills, lozenges or wafers, but in bizarre and unlikely devices, such as the 'electropoise', regularly advertised in the 1890s thus: 'a thermal instrument with an electrical force simulating the nervous current, and evidently acting through trophic nerves'. The electropoise consisted of wires attached to a metal cylinder, which was placed in water, while the wires were placed in contact with the patient's body. The exact nature of the force that flowed between water and patient remains to this day somewhat unclear, but it sounds more dangerous than healthy.

Perhaps it is not surprising that such inventions were accepted by a gullible minority of the Victorian population in an age when genuine scientific advances were astonishing the public. Towards the end of Victoria's reign, for example, a much more unbelievable discovery was widely publicized in the press. In 1896 it was claimed that there were rays that allowed a doctor to see through solid tissue. This was the remarkable discovery of 'Röntgen rays', which these days we call X-rays.

ALTERNATIVE THERAPIES

BATHING

Many Victorians believed that bathing was not only hygienic, but could increase one's vitality and even cure disease. Sea-water was particularly valued, and salt water was available in most London baths. *Mogg's New Picture of London* from 1844 gives the following price range for bathing: 'Cold bath, 1s.; warm bath, 3s.6d.; sea water, 3s.6d.; warm sea water, 7s.6d.' In addition to traditional baths, Turkish baths became increasingly popular from the 1860s onwards.

ELECTRICITY

'Faradic batteries', portable devices that supplied electric shocks to the body, were sold by mail-order companies who claimed that they cured most known ills.

HOMEOPATHY

Homeopathy (treating disease by administering small doses of drugs that produce similar symptoms) was introduced into Britain in the 1830s by Dr Frederick Quin, a friend of the rich and famous. The London Homeopathic Hospital was founded in 1849.

MESMERISM

Mesmerism was a form of hypnotism that was performed by waving one's hands near the subject; it was used to anaesthetize susceptible patients during the 1830s and

Below: The supposed life-giving properties of ozone.

Above: Turkish Baths at Bishopsgate.

1840s. Some, including Charles Dickens, even claimed illnesses could be cured by hypnotism. However, chemicals, such as ether and chloroform, were introduced in the mid-1840s, and when the London surgeon Robert Liston successfully used ether for an amputation in 1846 mesmerism lost many of its supporters.

OZONE

A visit to the seaside was often recommended by London doctors, not only as a break from busy city life but because, in addition to bathing, breathing ozone was commonly believed to boost one's health.

PILLS, LOZENGES AND WAFERS

Extravagant claims for patent medicinal products were peddled in newspaper and magazine advertisements throughout the Victorian era. 'Pulmonic Wafers' were marketed to cure asthma, consumption, influenza and coughs; the likes of 'Bourchardat's Gluten Bread, Chocolate and Semola' claimed to relieve not only diabetes but 'general debility' and consumption. Mineral waters were also consumed by many Victorians on health grounds; 'Pitkeathly Table Water', for instance, suggested it could act as a 'remedial agent in cases of Sluggish Liver, Plethoric States of the System, Chronic Affections of the Organs of Respiration and Circulation, Gastric Derangement and Biliousness'.

EDUCATION

SCHOOLBOYS

CITY OF LONDON SCHOOL...
Established 1835, for the sons of
respectable persons engaged in
professional, commercial or trading
pursuits... The school year is divided
into three terms... the charge for each
pupil is 2l. 5s a term. The printed form
of application for admission may be
had of the secretary, and must be filled
up by the parent or guardian, and
signed by a member of the Corporation
of London. The general course of
instruction includes the English, French,
German, Latin, and Greek Languages,
Writing, Arithmetic, Mathematics,
Book-keeping, Geography and History.

PETER CUNNINGHAM, *HAND-BOOK OF*
LONDON, 1850

A good education at the beginning of
Victoria's reign was largely the prerogative
of males from well-to-do families. Boys
would typically be educated at home by a
private tutor, and then sent to school,
whether a prestigious 'public school' (an
old endowed grammar school, not wholly dependent
on fees) or a private establishment. They would then
proceed to university. This would generally be either
Oxford or Cambridge, or, if one was not a member of
the Church of England, perhaps University College
London, which opened its doors to students in 1828
as a non-denominational alternative to Oxbridge.

Above: Christ's Hospital, otherwise known as the Blue Coat
School, was founded in 1553. The school relocated to Sussex
in 1902, and its ancient buildings were demolished.

Opposite: The City of London School was established in 1835
for the sons of 'respectable persons' engaged in trade. In 1883
it moved to this new building on the Victoria Embankment.

London's Public Schools

London had several well-regarded public schools,
including St Paul's School, the Merchant Taylors'
School, Charterhouse and Westminster. All were
ancient institutions: the Merchant Taylors' School,
for example, was founded in 1561, and it cost £12–16
per annum to send a child there in the nineteenth
century, which was the equivalent of the wages of a
well-paid maid-servant. It was a day school, although
special arrangements could be made for a few pupils
to live with approved families, and it accepted boys
between the ages of nine and fourteen, based on
recommendations from the Merchant Taylors'
Company, an ancient guild of the City of London.

Like most public schools, the Merchant Taylors'
School had a traditional curriculum. This consisted
principally of Latin and Greek, plus mathematics, which
had been added in the 1830s. Modern languages and
science were only added in the 1870s. Moreover, for
the first half of the century, this limited classics curriculum was mirrored by rather Spartan conditions, typical
of the period. Indeed, in the 1850s there were still
no desks at the Merchant Taylors' School, so pupils
wrote on slates on their knees; no lights, so they had to
supply their own wax candle, and they were were also
obliged to bring their own food for lunch.

Other new public schools existed in the capital,
but they were not considered quite as prestigious as

Above: The interior of the Merchant Taylors' School, which was founded in 1561. This school was based in Suffolk Lane in the City of London, then relocated to Charterhouse Square in 1875.

the likes of the Merchant Taylors'. The City of London School, for instance, was founded in 1835 for 'sons of respectable persons engaged in professional, commercial or trading pursuits', hence an unusual focus on mathematics, arithmetic and book-keeping in its curriculum, in addition to the classics. Its academic standards were probably equal to the old schools, but it did not cater for the aristocracy; for the well-bred did not wish to have any involvement with those in 'trade'. Thus it lacked the cachet of its more ancient rivals. The likes of the City of London School were also disadvantaged in that they could not draw upon a history of famous alumni, and, more importantly, a long list of valuable scholarships and 'exhibitions' that allowed many students to go on to Oxford or Cambridge at the school's expense.

Scholarship Boys

Indeed, schooling was expensive. For boys from 'respectable' families whose parents could not afford school fees, the only hope was attaining a scholarship. Some of the public schools themselves offered a few scholarships each year, and, furthermore, a handful of schools were run on a wholly charitable basis. The most famous example of the latter was the Christ's Hospital, or 'Blue Coat', School. Sited near Newgate Prison, this school was founded in 1553 and got its nickname from the student's distinctive uniform 'a blue coat or gown, a yellow petticoat… a red leather girdle round the waist, yellow stockings, a clergyman's band round the neck, and a flat black cap of woollen yarn, about the size of a saucer'. Here, as with many Victorian charities, admission was based on the personal recommendation of a governor, with the caveat that the boy was between eight and ten years of age, 'free from active disease, as well as from any physical defect which would render them unable to take care of themselves'. Also, their parents had to have insufficient income to educate them.

SCHOOLGIRLS

Teach young women from their childhood upwards that marriage is their single career, and it is inevitable that they should look upon every hour which is not spent in promoting this sublime end and aim as so much subtracted from life…. the universe to her is only a collection of rich bachelors in search of wives, and of odious rivals who are contending with her for one or more of these two wary prizes. She thinks of nothing except her private affairs. She is indifferent to politics, to literature – in a word, to anything that requires thought. She reads novels of a kind, because novels are all about Love, and love had once something to do with marriage, her own peculiar and absorbing business. Beyond this her mind does not stir.

THE SATURDAY REVIEW, 1867

While in the 1830s most boys from a good background were expected to attend a grammar school, most middle- and upper-class girls received their education at home, typically from a governess. Assuming a separate male tutor was not employed, the governess might also provide basic education for any male siblings who were not yet old enough to attend a grammar school.

Reading and writing were the fundamental skills the governess had to impart to both sexes, but for girls any additional education was likely to focus on 'accomplishments', such as embroidery, music, singing and painting. Traditionally, it was these feminine achievements that girls were expected to master, together with some basic mathematics that, for the middle-class girl at least, would allow her to undertake practical management of her household budget once she married. A girl might be sent out to school, but generally it was more a 'finishing school' than one devoted to academic excellence.

Above: Board Schools, which were introduced under the 1870 Education Act, offered reading and writing to all, and girls were often also taught household skills.
Below: Frances Buss (1827–94), a leading proponent of education for women, trained at Queen's College in 1849 before establishing the North London Collegiate School for Girls.

Widening Opportunities

A break with tradition began to occur in the mid-nineteenth century as more voices called for better education for women, with articles condemning the rather vacuous mind-set that concentration on accomplishments encouraged. A watershed was the founding in London of Queen's College in Harley Street in 1848, which taught 'arithmetic, drawing, English grammar, French, geography, history, Latin, vocal music, natural history, reading, writing'.

The College was founded to provide higher education for governesses, who the founders believed were often woefully ill-equipped to educate the children in their charge. The aim was also to raise the status of the governess – often a 'distressed gentlewoman', who was thrown into working life by force of circumstances, and generally under-

paid and ill-used by employers. Queen's College was swiftly followed by Bedford College in 1849, which provided similar lectures to those offered at Queen's.

The women educated in these two institutions went on to revolutionize education by creating new schools for girls, which they planned to turn into the equivalent to the boys' grammar schools in terms of educational achievement. Two such women were Frances Mary Buss, who founded the North London Collegiate School for Girls in 1850, and Dorothea Beale, who became Principal of Cheltenham Ladies College in 1858. Their example was followed by The Girls' Public Day School Company, founded in 1872, which had established over thirty girls' schools by the end of Victoria's reign.

Further Education for Women

At the same time as these academically challenging schools for girls appeared, higher education women entering the medical profession'), dispensing and nursing, cookery instructor (a National School of Cookery was established in Kensington in 1873, to train ladies in domestic science) and music.

Cassell's Household Guide also toyed with the possibility that women might one day consider becoming librarians, stating 'the Americans have already set us an example here, and in the Public Library at Boston, U.S., seventy ladies are employed, a few men only being kept to lift the heaviest books on the high shelves. The ladies appear to have given the utmost satisfaction in this position, to which they appear thoroughly suited.'

RAGGED SCHOOLS

RAGGED SCHOOL UNION…
was established in 1844, with the view of bringing a "plain" but sound education within the reach of even the very humblest classes, of providing them with gratuitous shelter from the inclemency of the weather, and stimulating them to industrial and prudent habits. These objects are provided for, as far as the resources of the society will allow, by ragged schools situated in the worst neighbourhoods of London… by penny banks connected with these schools… and by eight Shoe-Black brigades (distinguished each by a cheap coloured uniform), comprising some 350 boys… whose eager cry of, "Have your boots blacked, sir?—only one penny!" salutes the passer-by in every busy metropolitan thoroughfare. In certain localities Refuges have been established, which afford to destitute lads and girls a night's shelter and a good supper and breakfast. The society also interests itself in procuring employment for deserving industry, and in promoting the emigration of suitable persons.

CRUCHLEY'S LONDON IN 1865: *A HANDBOOK FOR STRANGERS*, 1865

Above: *Lambeth Ragged School for Girls was part of the Ragged School Union, a charity founded in 1844 devoted to educating the poorest in society.*

also began to change, with women's colleges appearing at Oxford – Lady Margaret Hall and Somerville in 1879 – and Cambridge – Girton in 1869 and Newnham in 1871 (although these two colleges were not officially associated with Cambridge University at first). In 1878 the University of London took a lead and actually admitted women to all its degree subjects, with the exception of the delicate area of medicine. Even this exception was overturned in 1879, when the London Medical College for Women was given degree-granting status by the University.

Yet, for all these improvements, even by the end of the century, it was a brave woman who pursued education with a view to a professional career, and her options were still very limited. *Cassell's Household Guide*, for example, summarized the potential vocations for women as the following: art employment, officials under local government and other boards, posts of superintendence, elementary teaching, high-class tuition, medicine ('whatever may be the opinion we individually hold upon the propriety of

If any group, apart from women, was denied an education at the start of Victoria's reign, it was the children of the poor. Generally, they were sent to work in factories or at manual occupations as soon as they were physically able; schooling was an expensive luxury. Nevertheless, there was a widespread desire to improve the situation. For, while many Victorians were equivocal about the benefits of education for women, there was greater agreement about the effects of lack of education among the poor.

Indeed, many arguments were put forward: that the common man, with no education, was only equipped to do manual labour, whereas employers increasingly wanted skilled and intelligent workers; that ignorance of religious teaching fostered immorality. It even was suggested, moreover, after the 1867 Reform Act granted more working men a right to vote, that it was important for the nation that the working classes understood the complexities of political issues.

Teaching the Disadvantaged

There was, in fairness, some basic educational provision for the poor in London at the start of the nineteenth century, though it was very basic indeed. Typically, it came in the form of private 'Dame Schools', thus named because they were run by elderly women. Charles Dickens described one such teacher in *Great Expectations* – 'a ridiculous old woman of limited means and unlimited infirmity, who used to go to sleep from six to seven every evening, in the society of youth who paid twopence per week each, for the improving opportunity of seeing her do it'. Many others referred to the schools in similar terms; often, they amounted to no more than child-care for working-class parents. Certainly they had limited educational value.

Slightly better than the Dame Schools were church schools. There were two major societies that established religious schools – the British and Foreign Schools Society (established 1814) which was non-conformist in character, and the National Society for Promoting the Education of the Poor in the Principles of the Established Church (established 1811) which was backed by the Church of England. There was a degree of religious rivalry between the two bodies, but they both provided a basic education of reading,

Above: *Formerly the largest Ragged School in London, the Copperfield Road School in Hackney opened in 1876, but now operates as a museum of Victorian schooling.*

writing and arithmetic. They were, however, reliant on the monitorial system, whereby children sat in massive classes and teaching was delegated to older boys known as monitors who did their best to pass on the lessons to their groups of charges. Individual attention was non-existent; rote learning was the norm and standards were fairly low, with the greatest emphasis generally placed on religious education.

In 1844, another group, the 'Ragged School Union' began its work, opening schools for those poorest children whose parents could not even afford the few pence required to send their offspring to the church schools. The Ragged School organization was

Above: Christ Church Primary School, Brick Lane, east London, is a church school that was built in 1873–4. Its unusual Gothic arches were constructed to avoid disturbing the ancient graveyard on which it is sited.

a charity not only concerned with schooling, but with improving the welfare of the very poorest in society.

By the middle of the century, however, there was a growing consensus that government should play more of a role in organizing education. One incentive for the government to step in was the series of Factories Acts (and similar measures) between the 1830s and 1860s, which limited the number of hours children could be employed and which resulted in increasing numbers of children forced onto the streets when not working. Another incentive was that the government had been providing grants to schools since 1833, yet it had had relatively little say in how they were run.

Education for All

Successive government administrations began to gain control of the educational system: Her Majesty's Inspectorate of Schools was set up in 1839, and in 1858 the Newcastle Commission was established to 'inquire into the present state of popular education in England, and to consider and report what measures, if any, are required for the extension of sound and cheap elementary instruction to all classes of the people'. The conclusions of the Commission led to the Revised Code of 1862, which established both attendance by pupils and satisfactory testing in reading, writing and arithmetic as the criteria for government grants. Religious knowledge was not included, as inter-denominational disputes made this too divisive.

Eight years later, the Education Act of 1870 was passed. It was a decisive measure, since it allowed for the creation of public 'School Boards' where provision by church schools was inadequate. In other words, state education was born. Funding was redirected to these new School Boards, sapping religious schools of their main income. Grants for teaching new examinable subjects were offered – English grammar, history, geography and science were gradually introduced – and in London attendance at school was made compulsory for five- to ten-year olds from 1880 onwards. But Board Schools could still charge parents up to 9d. a week, and many children were kept away because their parents could not pay this cost. Finally, in 1891, fees were abolished and attendance improved dramatically – free state education was available in the capital.

Of course, the new system was not perfect. Indeed, throughout the nineteenth century, the same issues argued about today – the importance of examinations, lack of resources, the relevance of statistics, the number of subjects taught, and so on – were all intensely debated. Attendance was, moreover, always an issue, even after 1891. Indeed, the London School Board employed a good number of 'School Board Visitors' who worked to seek out truants.

By the end of the century, the vast majority of young children attended school, whether in the church schools, which still provided about fifty per cent of teaching, or Board Schools. As the writer George Sims put it in 1889, 'now there is hardly a child above a certain age – no matter how wretched its conditions may be – that is not brought within the beneficial influence of education.'

Above: Board Schools took the poorest childen off the streets, which must have made an evident difference to the ordinary Londoner.

Below: This typical 1890s London Board School was designed with tall windows for maximum light and ventilation. As with many Victorian buildings, this has been converted into housing as children now go to much larger schools.

FURTHER EDUCATION

*The LONDON MECHANICS' INSTITUTION...
is the oldest, and, in fact, may be considered the
originator of all the Mechanics' or Popular
Institutes for education, literature, and science,
in England... Its library contains 4000 volumes.
There are reading-rooms, class-rooms, a capacious
"theatre" or lecture-room, in which for thirty-five
years the lectures have been given weekly...*

*Of a similar class are: The London Institution,
Finsbury Circus... the Crosby Hall Institute,
Bishopgate Street; the Southwark Institution,
Southwark Bridge Road; the Pimlico and
Belgravia Institute... the Russell Institution...
the Marylebone Institution... the Working Men's
College, Great Ormond Street, established by the
Rev. F.D. Maurice, and providing first-class
instruction for artisans, mechanics, and others,
in arithmetic, pure and mixed mathematics,
mechanics, English composition, drawing, book-
keeping, English history, &c., at a cost of from
2s. 6d. to 5s. per term of eight weeks.*

CRUCHLEY'S LONDON IN 1865: A HANDBOOK FOR
STRANGERS, 1865

*Above: The People's Palace was a free cultural centre in the
East End. It was opened in 1887 by Queen Victoria and by
the late 1890s boasted some 1.5 million visitors per year.*

Although the state supplied primary education up to
the age of twelve by 1899, there was no state provision for secondary education. The ethic of 'self-help'
(to quote the title of Samuel Smiles's bestseller of
that name, published in 1859) was, however, much
promoted, and many urged the working class to
'better themselves'.

Bettering Themselves

To encourage such efforts, numerous 'Working
Men's Institutions' were created by private
individuals or charitable bodies, beginning with the
Mechanics' Institute founded in 1823 – 'mechanic' in
this Victorian usage meaning manual labourer. These
institutions were built to provide educational support
for working men in the form of libraries,
lectures and lecture halls, mostly on a subscription
basis, with the emphasis on workplace-related knowledge, concentrating on science and engineering.

Few of the old Mechanics' Institutes still exist today,
but many of their successors, created in the second half

of the nineteenth century, have survived in one form or another. 'The 'People's Palace' in Mile End, for instance, founded in 1886, was built as a free cultural institute for the inhabitants of east London, and contained a library, lecture hall, swimming bath, gymnasium, winter garden and technical schools. The 'Palace' is now part of Queen Mary College, a college within the modern University of London.

Similarly, the Northampton Institute, based in Northampton Square, Clerkenwell, was founded in 1883 to promote the 'industrial skill, general knowledge, health and well-being of young men and women belonging to the poorer classes', with teaching available in 'Mechanical Engineering', 'Artistic Crafts', 'Electrical Engineering', 'Horology' (clock-making was a historic trade in the locality), 'Electro-Chemistry' and 'Domestic Economy and Women's Trades'; this institute is now City University.

The principal model for such late Victorian institutions was, however, the Regent Street Polytechnic. The Polytechnic began as an educational and entertainment venue in 1838 for 'the advancement of the Arts and Practical Science, especially in connection with Agriculture, Mining, Machinery, Manufactures, and other branches of industry'. Its principal attraction was a diving bell in which visitors could be submerged in a tank of water. In 1881, following a fire and financial problems, the Polytechnic was acquired by the philanthropist Quintin Hogg, who organized bible classes, social and athletic clubs and lectures, as well as technical training, for which he fostered educational links with commercial firms. The Polytechnic went on to become Westminster University.

Above: The Bishopsgate Institute, a charity founded by Rev. William Rogers in 1895, continues to provide a free library, concert hall and meeting rooms for local residents.

Lending Libraries

The Polytechnic did not, however, supply free education, and so excluded the very poor who could ill-afford fees for classes. Indeed, although a few institutions like The People's Palace were gratuitous, free educational resources only became

Above: *The Whitechapel Library in east London was originally one of the many public libraries financed by the philanthropist John Passmore Edwards (1823–1911).*

Left: *The London Library was founded by the writer and critic Thomas Carlyle in 1841 when he became dissatisfied with the service at the library of the British Museum.*

commonplace in the capital with the appearance of public libraries – and they were a long time coming.

For much of the century, the only public libraries in London were subscription libraries – such as the scholarly London Library in St James's Square, founded in 1841, or the more general Mudie's of New Oxford Street, founded in 1842. The Library Act of 1850 allowed for the creation of public libraries, but its formulation did not allow most local authorities to raise sufficient funds. Westminster built the first public library in London in Great Smith Street in 1857, but for many districts it was only when philanthropists stepped in that free public libraries were founded. The first in east London was the Whitechapel Library, opened in 1892, with funds from the philanthropist John Passmore Edwards, editor of the journal *Building News*. The sugar magnate Henry Tate followed suit in 1893 with libraries in Battersea, Brixton and Streatham. Many of these institutions are still in use today.

RAGGED SCHOOLS

The Ragged School Union was founded in 1844, with the object of providing free education for the poorest children in society. Lessons included basic reading, writing, arithmetic and scripture, and sometimes 'industrial classes' teaching skills like tailoring, needlework and shoe-making. Teaching children from the slums of London was, however, not an easy task, as one teacher reported in 1850:-

28 October, 1849

We prepared the school by placing benches in situations for the division of the scholars into four classes, and as they came tumbling and bawling up the stairs, we directed them to seats.

In mere schooling they are not behindhand, but in decency of behaviour or in respect for the teacher, or in discipline of any kind, they are totally unparalleled. No school can possibly be worse than this. It were an easier task to get attention from savages.

They require more training than teaching.

To compose the children, I proposed that we should have a little music – the first verse of the Evening Hymn. We then invited the children to follow us, and we got through the first line or two very well, but a blackguard boy thought proper to set up on his own account, and he led off a song in this strain:-

*"Oh, Susanah,
don't you cry for me,
I'm off to Alabama,
With a banjo on my knee!"*

I need scarcely add that every boy followed this leader – aye, girls and all – and I could not check them.

In the midst of the Lord's Prayer, several shrill cries of "cat's meat" and "mew, mew".

All our copy books have been stolen, and proofs exist that the school is used at night as a sleeping-room. We must get a stronger door to it.

31 October, 1849

It is apparently worse than useless to expect a man to be made better by merely learning to read and write. Those of our scholars who can do so best are decidedly the most depraved.

There is a boy in my first class who has made as much as fourteen pence a week by writing begging letters, for his neighbours, for which he charged one penny a piece; and he also receives a few coppers now and then from the coster-mongers, who employ him to conduct their business correspondence. His moral tone is exceedingly low.

'DIARY OF A RAGGED SCHOOL TEACHER',
English Journal of Education, 1850.

HOUSING

FASHIONABLE LONDON

Mayfair,—strictly the immediate neighbourhood of Berkeley-square, but commonly known as the district lying between Park-lane, Piccadilly, Bond-street, and Brook-street, is still, from the society point of view, the crème de la crême *of residential London. The smallest and most inconvenient house—and it still contains many to which the term "house" is barely applicable but by courtesy—lets readily at a rent which, in less sought-after neighbourhoods, would provide a handsome establishment.*

CHARLES DICKENS JR, *DICKENS'S DICTIONARY OF LONDON*, 1879

The most exclusive residential areas of the Victorian capital were Mayfair and Belgravia. There were prosperous families living elsewhere in the metropolis, but the West End had a certain cachet about it, which, for example, Bloomsbury never quite acquired. Mayfair, lying between Park Lane and Regent's Street, was built up in the eighteenth century, with grand townhouses for the aristocracy, centred round three great squares (Grosvenor, Berkeley and Hanover). Even today, the district retains a Georgian feel. Belgravia, centred round Belgrave Square, was developed in the 1820s under the auspices of Thomas Cubitt. A renowned builder, Cubitt also oversaw the construction of Gordon and Tavistock squares in Bloomsbury in the same decade, and the development of Pimlico in the 1830s.

Status Accorded by Street

This is not to say that Mayfair and Belgravia were equals. Houses in particular streets and squares implied differing degrees of social standing. Certainly, despite Cubitt's fame and the grandeur of Belgrave Square's neo-classical

terraces, the newly built district never gained quite the same aristocratic reputation as its older neighbour. In fact, although their houses were equally impressive, and often cost as much to rent as those in Mayfair, the inhabitants of Belgravia were more likely to be, to quote *Dickens's Dictionary of London* of 1879, 'the large and rapidly-increasing class of

Opposite: The small-scale housing development of Holly Village in Hampstead was built in 1865 to an elaborate Gothic design by Henry Darbishire.

Below: The grand neo-classical terraces of Eaton Square in Belgravia were intended to appeal to the wealthiest members of Victorian society.

wealthy persons who live in town all the year round'. In other words, Belgravia became home to the *nouveaux riches*, families of rich merchants or bankers who lacked a country estate or simply chose to ignore the traditional 'season' – the upper-class custom of spending summer at one's town house in London attending society gatherings and spending the rest of the year in the country.

Many of their grand town houses survive to this day, and both Mayfair and Belgravia remain decidedly upmarket areas. However, appearances are a little deceptive, since few of these mansions remain intact as individual homes. Most have been split into flats or refurbished as embassies or office space, victims of changing economic realities, not least the decline in the availability of servants during the twentieth century.

Below: Service was the largest employer of women through-out the nineteenth century. A wealthy family living in a large town house could easily employ a dozen servants.

THE NEW COOK.

Upstairs Downstairs

Even for their original occupiers, the major overhead involved in renting or owning such a home was the cost of employing servants. A substantial town house in Belgravia ranged over six floors, including the attic (generally servants' quarters) and the basement (kitchen, scullery, pantry), and was designed on the premise that staff were continually available to distribute coal, water and food, which were brought up from the basement.

The availability of indoor plumbing from the mid-nineteenth century undoubtedly lightened some of this burden, but there were countless other arduous tasks, not least the constant cleaning of the house and household objects, which required a great deal of manpower. A wealthy household typically employed a cook, kitchenmaid, one or two housemaids and lady's maids, a butler, footman, coachman and, perhaps, even a stable-boy, as most families would also keep a carriage in a nearby mews.

Servants' Quarters

The servants of Mayfair and Belgravia did not, naturally, reside in the same luxury as their employers, even though they might live under the same roof. Domestic staff could, at least, rely on a clean attic room to sleep in, with decent bed and bedding, but they would frequently have to share. Moreover, their bedrooms were often kept deliberately poorly furnished and unhomely, with many advice manuals warning householders of the dangers of 'luxury' and 'indulgence'. Such Spartan conditions, it was claimed, were still better than what a servant might expect if he or she were not in service. Indeed, this was true, and doubtless many servants did consider themselves lucky.

Outside the town house, things were generally somewhat worse. The mews homes of coachmen and their families, small dingy rooms above stables, were notoriously poor and, of course, odorous. Dickens, for example, in *Little Dorrit*, described a typical Mayfair mews as 'a hideous little street of dead wall, stables, and dunghills'.

The mews of Mayfair and elsewhere were cleverly concealed: just as the movement of indoor servants was, wherever possible, kept to discrete back stairs, so the messy business of maintaining a coach and horses was carried out in discrete back streets. A good many such streets still survive, the stables converted into flats and houses, a reminder not only of the importance of horse power in the Victorian period, but of the hidden infrastructure that supported the grand West End mansions.

Although Mayfair and Belgravia were the playgrounds of the rich, the poor were never that far away. John Hollingshead writing in his campaigning pamphlet 'Ragged London in 1861', stated that 'From Belgravia to Bloomsbury – from St Pancras to Bayswater – there is hardly a settlement of leading residences that has not its particular colony of ill-housed poor hanging on to its skirts'. These 'ill-housed poor', found in the back streets, were the providers of groceries, the workmen, the charwomen and the laundresses who all made a living by supplying the well-off, both middle and upper classes, with goods and services. In turn, local public houses, pawnbrokers, chandlers and countless others provided their services to these 'hangers-on'. Thus, even in fashionable London, rich and poor lived in relative intimacy with each other, even if the former were somewhat loath to acknowledge it.

Above: Behind many town houses were mews streets, which housed not only horses, but coachmen and their families, too.

MODEL HOUSING

The Metropolitan Association for Improving the Dwellings of the Industrious Classes was incorporated by royal charter in 1845, and seems destined to carry out in the highest degree the aims and intentions of the benevolent party who first attempted the bettering of the prospects of working men. This association is established on a principle which, in this business-like age, is sure to be duly appreciated... namely, that of an investment of capital, with a prospect of a fair return. It is, in fact, a commercial speculation of a very safe and honourable kind... The first buildings erected by this association were those in the Old St. Pancras Road... These were arranged to accommodate 110 families, and were opened to the tenants in 1848. They have been constantly occupied since their completion, to the great advantage and improved health of the inmates.

THE PICTORIAL HANDBOOK OF LONDON, 1854

The living conditions of the poor, whether Hollingshead's 'hangers-on', factory workers or the idle unemployed, were of considerable interest to Victorian social reformers. By the mid-nineteenth century, there was a growing consensus that housing for the working classes had to be improved, and an acknowledgement of the 'physical and moral evils' attendant upon slum dwellings, in which many working men were forced to live in.

Slums and Ghettoes

In areas such as the notorious Seven Dials, near Covent Garden, conditions were atrocious. Charles Dickens described the district as containing 'wretched houses with broken windows patched with rags and paper; every room let out to a different family, and in many instances to two or even three... filth everywhere'. There were many such areas dotted throughout the Great Metropolis. Some were well known, such as Seven Dials and St Giles, whereas others, equally bad, were familiar only to the local inhabitants and visiting charity workers.

Admittedly, there had always been slums in London, but new factors came into play during the nineteenth century. One problem, ironically enough, was slum clearances, carried out in preparation for the building of new roads and railways, which increased

Above: 'Rent Day' (Punch, 1850) shows life in a rented cellar room, which also served as a makeshift stable.

Below: 'A Court for King Cholera' (Punch, 1852) depicts a poverty-stricken London courtyard, with lodgings and 'good beds' available in ramshackle houses. Note the children are playing around a dung-heap.

years, the number of Londoners had quadrupled, rising to over 4.5 million inhabitants by 1901. Immigration played a substantial role: famine and poverty drove a million people from Ireland in the 1840s, many of whom settled in London; likewise, over a hundred thousand Jewish immigrants enlarged the existing East End Jewish community towards the end of Victoria's reign, escaping hardship and persecution in eastern Europe. Most significantly, throughout the century, many thousands came from rural England in search of work.

The result was that the poor were packed tighter and tighter into the city's slums and landlords exploited the demand for accommodation with ruthless efficiency. Rooms were divided and subdivided; cellars and attics were found to easily support a family or two and no consideration was given to sanitation. The supply of such housing, even the leasing of shared rooms in crumbling tenements, was a very profitable business.

the demand for the remaining low-rent properties. Moreover, there was simply a massive increase in London's population: within a span of a hundred

Housing the Poor

A first attempt to address the problem was made, in typical Victorian fashion, not by the government but by the private efforts of individuals and charities. Their efforts were intended to show the way forward through the construction of 'model housing' – new, clean and sanitary lodging-houses and homes – for rent by workers as opposed to the destitute or very poor; they belonged in the workhouse or had to fend for themselves.

This concept of providing special housing for the working poor was an innovative idea. Previously, in central London at least, housing was rarely built with the lower classes in mind. For there was less profit to be made from the rents of numerous ill-paid workers than from a few reliable middle-class families in middle-class homes. Consequently, the poor tended to congregate in areas that had long since become run down, often in old and decrepit houses, formerly the property of the middle classes. Moreover, if new housing was built, it was often makeshift, in areas considered unlikely to attract the better off. In both cases, slums were the result. The only exception to such conditions was the capital's ancient almshouses, built by individual patrons for aged or infirm dependants in previous centuries. Many still survive today, such as the buildings of the Geffrye Museum in Hackney, but they were not an adequate solution to nineteenth-century problems.

Above: Almshouses, such as these in Hackney, built in 1714 for some fifty residents, housed the aged or infirm in the early nineteenth century; they now house the Geffrye Museum.

It was The Society for Improving the Condition of the Labouring Classes that took the lead, by creating 'Model Housing' in central London. Founded in 1844, the society boasted the Queen and Prince Albert as patrons and Lord Shaftesbury as Chairman. It built or reconstructed a small number of 'Lodging-Houses for Working Men', ensuring the dormitories were whitewashed and kept clean, and provided adequate cooking and washing facilities. Today, this sounds like an insignificant achievement, but the model lodgings were a stark contrast to the dirt-ridden, insect-infested, ill-ventilated dens found elsewhere in London. Likewise, The Metropolitan Association for Improving the Dwellings of the Industrious Classes was founded in the following year, 1845. It included in its showcase St Pancras buildings a wash-house and baths, a coffee room, a reading room and a cook-shop, not to mention running water, lavatories and gas lighting.

Both these organizations had to campaign to find funding and were relatively small scale (the latter body only housed a thousand or so families by the late 1870s). Money, on the other hand, was not a

Above: *This 1870s Peabody Housing Trust building in Blackfriars was built to an austere-looking Italianate design of Henry Darbishire's, and is typical of Peabody housing.*

Left: *The flats of the Boundary Estate in east London were built between 1893 and 1900 to rehouse 5,000 people. They were among the first social housing to be developed by the newly formed London County Council.*

problem for the American businessman and philanthropist, George Peabody, who left a legacy of a self-perpetuating £500,000 fund to provide cheap housing for the London poor, beginning with a project in Spitalfields, which opened in 1864. His blocks of flats can still be seen throughout the capital and, though somewhat barrack-like in design, they provide housing for many modern Londoners. The Peabody Housing Trust continues to develop social housing throughout the capital today.

Spreading the Support Network

Although the first 'model housing' projects concentrated on the centre of London, poor housing conditions were not limited to the central slums.

Hector Gavin's 1840s investigation into Bethnal Green in east London, for example, found that the 'cottages' of the district were 'constructed in defiance of every law and principle on which the health and lives of the occupants depend,' lacking adequate foundations, drainage and ventilation.

Consequently, during the 1860s and 1870s, the proponents of 'model housing' turned their attention to this problem. They focused on the new working-class suburbs that were developing around railway lines and manufacturing plants, previously on the fringes of the growing metropolis. These were districts like Stratford and Bow in the east, or Battersea in the south, where workers were flocking in their thousands. In particular, the Artizans, Labourers' and General Dwellings Company was founded in 1867, 'for the erection of improved dwellings near to the great centres of industry, but free from the annoyances arising from the proximity of manufactures'.

Below: Fifth Avenue in Queen's Park, which was completed in 1881, consists of plain two-storey terraces, with the exception of the turreted corner houses, which provide a Gothic touch.

The idea behind the Dwellings Company was not to build Peabody-style flats, but 'cottage estates' of well-constructed two-storey terraces. The first estate was built in Shaftesbury Park, Battersea, between 1872 and 1877. The second development was Queen's Park, West Kilburn, constructed between 1875 and 1881. An indication of the intended moral, orderly nature of the estates can be gleaned from the prohibition of public houses, and, in the case of Queen's Park, the New York-style 'grid' approach to street names. The area still possesses a First, Second, Third, Fourth, Fifth and Sixth Avenue, and intersecting streets were originally named 'A' through to 'P'.

It was only in the 1890s that local government finally took responsibility for housing, with local authorities having been given powers under the Artisan's Dwelling Act 1875 and the Housing of the Working Classes Act 1890 to clear slums and relocate residents into what we now call council housing. The first area in London to benefit was on the borders of Bethnal Green, with the notorious Old Nichol slum replaced by the Boundary Estate, whose buildings still provide social housing today.

SUBURBIA

At Turnham Green, close by the railway-station, an important building enterprise is in progress on the Bedford Park estate, the architect being Mr. R. Norman Shaw. Some two hundred houses are erected, at rentals varying from 40l. to 120l. per annum. Several valuable suggestions of Dr. Richardson are being carried out on this estate, which also offers a club for the use of the residents. The projectors state in their prospectus, 'It is believed that this estate represents the first endeavour to secure, in the erection of houses at moderate rents, good construction, with attention to artistic effect, coupled with most complete sanitary arrangements, both in their drainage and perfect freedom from sewer gas.'

THE SUBURBAN HOMES OF LONDON, 1881

Opposite: The houses in Phillimore Gardens, Kensington were built in 1858 and were rather exclusive, costing the princely sum of £250–£500 a year to rent in the 1880s.

Below: The typical suburban terrace of Clapton Passage in Hackney was built in 1882 for the average middle-class family, and a house here would have cost £45–£75 a year to rent.

While the upper classes had large town houses and country estates, and the working man could aspire to a decent worker's cottage in Battersea or Queen's Park, the middle classes sought out suburbia. Indeed, the creation of a great ring of commuter suburbs round the centre of London was one of the most remarkable physical changes that took place in the Victorian capital. Admittedly, it was a change that was not universally admired. Many found it shocking how quickly the countryside that surrounded the metropolis could become desolate 'brick-fields'. The same pattern was repeated again and again: land was purchased, plots were staked out and the London clay was excavated and fired in kilns to make bricks, as foundations were laid for new buildings and roads. Familiar green fields seemed to vanish almost over night, under 'a mantle of red brick', as vast suburbs were created piecemeal by speculative builders.

Row upon Row

The new suburbs swiftly engulfed what were once relatively isolated communities on the edge of the city. A few areas survived this transition quite well. Hampstead, once a country retreat for wealthy Londoners, was one district to be built up during the nineteenth century. Yet, today, it still possesses a semi-rural atmosphere, and contains many historic properties. It also benefits from its proximity to Hampstead Heath, an ancient wooded common, which was only saved from builders after an extensive public campaign. Likewise, nearby Highgate can still lay claim to a semblance of rusticity.

It is much more difficult, on the other hand, to envisage modern 'inner city' areas, such as Notting Hill in west London and Brixton in south London, as quiet villages that once existed on the very outskirts of the capital. Some places are even entirely lost, surviving only in street names. How many modern Londoners, for instance, could locate the old hamlet of Shacklewell? Shacklewell Green, once the heart of a thriving community, is now little more than a small traffic island in the borough of Hackney.

What drove the middle classes into the suburbs? It was not home ownership, as they still rented their homes from rich landlords who bought the new properties. In short, they

Above: Bedford Park in Turnham Green, west London, was an Arts and Crafts housing development. This house in Priory Avenue was built to the designs of E.J. May in 1880.

simply wanted somewhere free from the noise and pollution of the city, but with the advantages and amenities of the city near at hand. And, by the 1880s there were many suburban areas one might choose from, if one worked in central London and had a decent income.

Some districts were 'commutable' merely by omnibus and tram, like Holloway in north London; others, further afield, relied on commuters utilizing the growing network of railways. Indeed, the railways meant suburbanites could travel considerable distances. *The Suburban Homes of London*, for instance, a guidebook for prospective buyers published in 1881, includes areas as disparate as Northolt in the west, Croydon in the south and Wanstead in the east, places that still entail a substantial commute into central London today.

Following a Pattern

Some critics objected to the architectural monotony and relentless creep outwards of the new suburbs. In fact, George Cruikshank, the celebrated artist,

famously drew a cartoon of the 'march of bricks and mortar', encroaching on semi-rural Islington, as early as 1829.

However, although many suburbs were uniform, with most houses based upon standard plans and architect's pattern-books, there was an exception. Bedford Park in Turnham Green first built up during the 1870s and 1880s. It differed from previous suburban projects in that pre-eminent architects of the period, including Richard Norman Shaw, designed many of its houses individually, in the new 'Queen Anne' style, specifically for the site. Trees and greenery were incorporated and emphasized, rather than cleared, in Shaw's layout of the area, and the development was cleverly marketed as an 'aesthetic' rural enclave. The houses, in turn, eschewed the gloomier features of Victorian design: basements, for instance, were excluded and white palisade fences often replaced traditional iron-railings.

In consequence, Bedford Park was universally hailed as a great architectural achievement by contemporary critics. It has also been widely perceived, by modern commentators, as the prototype of the 'garden suburb', though, sadly, the area is now surrounded by less aesthetic twentieth-century suburban sprawl.

LOW-RISE LONDON

"They used to say," he continued, "an Englishman's house is his castle; and a good old-fashioned proverb it was in those days, when we looked down on the foreigner who preferred living under the same roof as a dozen others, to having a snug little house of his own in the suburbs. What is the cause of this change in the Englishman's way of living?"

GEORGE SALA, *LONDON UP TO DATE*, 1895

For much of the nineteenth century, the flip-side of the middle-class Victorian's aspiration to live in a suburban house was a concomitant loathing of the European solution to crowded urban spaces – the flat. Was this simply British conservatism? Perhaps.

It is worth noting that there were substantial inno-

Below: *Artillery Mansions in Westminster (built 1895) is an early example of purpose-built flats. The block includes a remarkable three-storey-high Gothic archway.*

vations in the Victorian period relating to housing. Putting aside changes in interior design pertaining to specific fashions, we might note that the nineteenth century saw the introduction of indoor plumbing (in upper-class homes at least – the lower classes generally made do with chamber pots and privies throughout the century) and that the concept of having a separate 'bathroom' gained currency from the middle of the century onwards. Equally, gas lighting replaced or, rather, supplemented the traditional candle and oil-lamp, and from the 1880s gas was slowly replaced with electricity.

Taking a broader view, it could also be argued that Bedford Park provided a novel template for many twentieth-century suburbs. Likewise, London's various model housing projects paved the way for the twentieth-century 'council estate' and high-density local authority housing. The Victorians were not averse to change.

ACCOMMODATION

RENTS (*Prices given weekly for easy comparison, though rent of a whole house was generally per annum, or possibly for the summer 'season' if in the West End.*)

A furnished house in the West End   5–25 guineas
(*Murray's Handbook to London As It Is*, 1879)
'Elegantly furnished rooms' in West End 4–15 guineas
(*Murray's Handbook to London As It Is*, 1879)
An unfurnished house in Holland Park   7–10 guineas
(*The Suburban Homes of London*, 1881)
A sitting room and bedroom in Pimlico   1–4 guineas
(*Murray's Handbook to London As It Is*, 1879)
A house in suburban Walthamstow   10–40 shillings
(*The Suburban Homes of London*, 1881)
Two rooms in Peabody Model Dwellings 4 shillings, 9d.
(*Dickens's Dictionary of London*, 1879)

HOTELS

Bed and breakfast, with coffee and cold meat; dinner, with soup and joint; and 'attendance' at the Midland Grand Hotel
14 shillings per night
(*Dickens's Dictionary of London*, 1879)
Bed and breakfast at a City 'boarding-house'
3 shillings per night
(*Cruchley's London*, 1865)
Bed in shared room in 'low lodging-house'
1–4d. per night
(*London Labour and the London Poor*, 1851)

Lowering Standards?

Yet, for all that, purpose-built flats, which were an obvious solution to an overcrowded city full of expensive properties, seemed to many well-to-do Londoners an innovation too far. Indeed, they only began to become popular among the middle and upper classes in the last two decades of the century, and many of the older generation still looked on them with distrust.

One reason for this aversion was the Continental associations of the 'flat' – quite simply, it did not seem a 'London' way of living. Another problem was that existing properties occupied by multiple persons and families were generally the homes of the poor or of the struggling artisan. Purpose-built apartments containing several planned rooms were different, but it was a hard association to dispel. Flats, worst of all, resembled the new 'model housing' of the working class. There was even concern expressed by some commentators about the dangers of mixing the social classes within an apartment building; different levels of society were in danger of being forced into contact with each other on communal stairs and landings.

It is also easy to forget how peculiar large apartment blocks must have looked to Victorian Londoners, since London was very much a low-rise city of relatively small buildings, with church steeples still providing highly visible landmarks and St Paul's dominating the skyline. Indeed, though they hardly compared to the sort of structures being erected in American cities at the same time, there was considerable comment on the 'monster' office buildings, flats and hotels that were finally constructed in London in the 1880s and 1890s.

In particular, after an early monolithic and notoriously ugly effort at a large apartment block – Queen Anne's Mansions, near St James's Park (completed 1889, demolished 1971) – which was a mere 14 storeys high, London County Council was prompted to establish bylaws limiting the height of buildings in the capital. It was said that Queen Anne's Mansions overshadowed the historic buildings of St James's and intruded upon the Queen, as residents had a view of the gardens of Buckingham Palace.

Times, of course, have changed. According to the 2001 census, forty-six per cent of the residents of Inner London now live in purpose-built flats.

Right: A mid-Victorian parlour as reconstructed in the Geffrye Museum. Over the following twenty years, Victorian rooms became darker and more cluttered.

HOME SWEET HOME

This is the true nature of home – it is the place of Peace; the shelter, not only from all injury, but from all terror, doubt, division. In so far as it is not this, it is not home; so far as the anxieties of the outer life penetrate into it, the inconsistently-minded, unknown, unloved, or hostile society of the outer world is allowed by either husband or wife to cross the threshold, it ceases to be home; it is then only a part of that outer world which you have roofed over and lifted fire in.

JOHN RUSKIN, *SESAME AND LILIES*, 1897

Another reason many middle-class Victorians disliked flats was the importance of 'home' in the Victorian imagination, which was perceived as an isolated sanctuary protecting its inhabitants from the demands of the outside world. A property that was shared with strangers, in any way, could not be home in the truest sense. Indeed, foreigners who visited London remarked on the English obsession with isolation. Max Schlesinger, a German writing in the 1850s, wrote of a 'mania for fortification', comparing the traditional London house with a castle, with its speared, iron railings as outer defences, and its steps over the basement 'area' like a draw-bridge over a moat.

Security Measures

In fairness, some of the 'fortified' features typical of London homes were quite practical. Spiked railings outside the property and wooden shutters inside the house, which could be closed and barred behind windows, were practical protection against burglary. Likewise, although thick, multi-layered damask curtains provided an opportunity for fashionable display, they also provided insulation and some protection from the encroachments of London's notoriously foggy and odoriferous atmosphere.

Nevertheless, such barriers clearly also sated the Victorian desire for privacy and for clear demarcation

Above: The Victorians occasionally toyed with Egyptian elements in their architecture. Richmond Avenue, Islington, is a notable example, with sphinxes guarding its houses.
Below: The satirical magazine Punch *took great pleasure in pointing out the follies of some Victorian fashions, such as aquarium-keeping.*

between work life and home life and between the respective spheres of men and women. For most contemporary social commentators, such as John Ruskin (1819–1900), agreed that a man's role was as 'the doer, the creator, the discoverer, the defender' – in other words, the breadwinner – whereas a woman's role was 'for sweet ordering, arrangement, and decision' – in other words, the homemaker. This did not mean that middle-class women were expected to besmirch themselves with the manual labour involved in keeping a home; rather, the mistress of the house was supposed to manage servants and household finances. It was a woman's nature and duty to stay at home and create a sanctuary for her husband and children, separate from 'the anxieties of outer life'.

A Busy House

What was that sanctuary like, behind its defences? It is impossible to chronicle every feature, but, certainly, the average middle-class house was unlike its modern counterpart in various ways. We have already mentioned nineteenth-century plumbing and lighting. Heating, of course, was based around coal fires. This required a good deal of fetching and carrying coals, maintenance of fireplaces, removing the accumulation of coal dust in the house; moreover, it demanded the services of one servant or more.

As for internal layout, kitchens generally boasted additional small rooms that have since become redundant, such as a separate pantry for keeping food cool, a scullery for washing up and other dirty tasks and a store for coal.

A Full House

In terms of decoration, there was considerable variation according to class, period and personal taste. Nonetheless, what is probably most striking to modern eyes, looking at Victorian drawings or photographs, is the difference between the archetypal middle-class Victorian parlour or drawing-room – which was generally speaking the best-kept room in the house and used to receive guests – and the modern 'living room'. In particular, wall-space in the mid-Victorian parlour was typically covered in numerous framed pictures and, later in the century, photographs. The result was that much of the wall was often obscured, even after patterned wallpaper became popular and affordable during the 1850s.

As the century progressed, furniture became bulkier and more padded, emphasizing comfort and stability, while drapes and curtains were heavy. Mantelpieces and other surfaces were covered in knick-knacks and bric-à-brac, such as statuettes, china, fans and seashells. A growing interest in natural history led to many homeowners having ferns or stuffed animals under protective glass domes for inspection. Likewise, there was something of a craze for aquariums. Finally, the focal point of the Victorian drawing room was the hearth or a central table – as opposed to today's usual television in a corner of the room.

The proliferation of objets d'art in Victorian drawing rooms was partly the result of a desire to show off the range of a family's taste and possessions, and to impress one's acquaintances when they visited. Today, it might be argued, we use gadgets, stereos, computers and so on, in smaller numbers, to fulfil a similar purpose. Another reason for such multiplicity was the fact that, unlike modern society, Victorians were loath to throw out the contents of a room and redecorate from scratch; household goods and furniture were intended to last a lifetime, and had a tendency to accumulate.

This superfluity of objects only began to disappear, in some homes at least, from the 1870s, not least because of the influence of the Arts and Crafts and Aesthetic movements, with people such as designer and craftsman William Morris (1834–96) and dramatist Oscar Wilde (1854–1900) advising the public on matters of taste in interior decoration. In particular, a

Above: *By the 1880s, the Oriental influence had pervaded many Victorian drawing rooms; note the blue-and-white tiling, the vases and the peacock feathers – all features beloved of the the Aesthetic Movement.*

new 'Oriental' look was promoted, with exotic Eastern goods available from new department stores such as Liberty, which was founded in London in 1875. In more daring homes, bamboo matting and Japanese vases replaced heavy rugs and stuffed animals. However, the new Aesthetic style also attracted a good deal of mockery in *Punch* and elsewhere, and in many houses the cluttered Victorian parlour persisted long into the twentieth century.

SHOPPING

explicitly, separating the 'Nobility and Gentry' of Mayfair from the workers and tradesmen of Soho. It continued to be much admired by the Victorians, who often referred to it as 'the finest thoroughfare in London'. Bond Street and Regent Street were the prime shopping locations for the well-to-do 'carriage trade' – the wealthy who would park their carriage outside a favourite shop and have shop assistants bring them samples of goods to look at.

The Victorians did, however, make their own mark on the street, albeit a destructive one. In 1848, Nash's 'Quadrant' of covered arcades outside the shops, on either side of the south part of the street, was demolished; it was said that the colonnades cast too large a shadow over the shops beneath and that prostitutes were liable to loiter in the Quadrant's shady confines.

Oxford Street, on the other hand, was not built according to any unified scheme, and did not have the aristocratic reputation of Regent Street; nor did it attract the same sort of shop. According to *Dickens's Dictionary of London*, (1879) it contained 'many houses which even in a third-rate street would be considered mean and unworthy of the place', and possessed an 'incongruity and diversity of architecture and appearance'.

Certainly, another look at Tallis's directories shows that in the early years of Victoria's reign, Nash's grand road boasted an *Artiste en Cheveux* (one assumes a rather high-class hairdresser), sellers of pomade and

Above: James Smith & Sons Umbrellas has been on New Oxford Street since 1857. Its large plate-glass windows for displaying goods were a Victorian innovation.

pomatum (beauty products), and numerous milliners – all catering to fashionable females. Oxford Street, meanwhile, had nothing quite so fancy, with, in addition to its many drapers, rather more lowly traders, such as butchers and cheesemongers. Yet, as the nineteenth century progressed, several of those drapers began to expand to take in larger premises and larger ranges of products. Thus stores like John Lewis and the now defunct Marshall and Snelgrove (taken over by Debenhams), turned into the department stores that still define the character of the street today.

A Lone Survivor

Unfortunately, few of the Victorian shop fronts of Regent Street and Oxford Street (and even fewer interiors) have weathered the commercial pressures of the last hundred years unscathed. In fact, it is on New Oxford Street, a road built in 1847 primarily to clear local slums and allow traffic to pass eastwards from Oxford Street, that one of the best examples of a Victorian shop remains – James Smith & Sons, Umbrellas. The firm has been in its present location at Hazelwood House since 1857, and is remarkably unchanged, both inside and out.

DEPARTMENT STORES

Nearly all the great shops in London are becoming vast stores... Many more people than formerly come to London, and to the large centres to do their shopping; they prefer to make their purchases where they can concentrate their forces and diminish fatigue... What an amount of trouble and expense is avoided where one can order one's New Zealand mutton downstairs, buy one's carpet on the ground floor, and deck oneself out in all the glory of Worth or La Ferrier, on the top floor...

FORTNIGHTLY REVIEW, JANUARY 1896

The journey from the small specialist store, like James Smith & Sons, to the modern department store is principally a story of small businesses that expanded during the later part of the nineteenth century, recognizing the commercial benefits of providing different product ranges under one roof. Harrods, for instance, is one famous example of this principle in action. The store began as a grocer's on the Brompton Road in 1849, and grew to meet the needs of the expanding well-to-do suburb of Kensington – a rural area at the start of the nineteenth century and a large urban development by the end – then the needs of London and even further afield.

The expansion of Harrods was also fuelled by the boom in tourism after the Great Exhibition, International Exhibition and their ilk, as the store was located just south of Hyde Park. For many stores, however, improvements in public transport were more important, as new train and omnibus routes allowed shoppers from both old and new suburbs easy access to shops in the city centre.

The Whiteleys Phenomenon

Just as today we see shopping centres spring up alongside major motorways, Victorian department stores were always well placed for public transport. This could mean simply ensuring a spot on Oxford Street, with its pre-existing transport infrastructure, or choosing somewhere further afield that was a growing suburb or likely to be developed. It is no coincidence, for example, that William Whiteley's fancy goods shop, which would become, arguably, the most famous department store in Victorian London, was founded in Westbourne Grove in 1863, shortly after the nearby Metropolitan Line underground station was opened at Paddington.

Initially, the ambitious retailer, having saved £700 from previous employment, merely opened a small draper's shop, where he sold ribbons, lace, trimmings and fancy goods. Within a year, Whiteley had fifteen assistants; in 1867 he went into silks, linens, mantles, drapery, dresses, millinery, haberdashery, ladies outfitting, gloves, hosiery, jewellery, furs, umbrellas; in 1870, having bought properties on either side of his original store, which was a common

Below: The Victorian exterior of Harrods – the world-famous department store which started out as a small grocers on the busy thoroughfare of Knightsbridge in 1849.

LONDON'S VICTORIAN MARKETS

Bermondsey Leather Market, Weston Street
The Bermondsey area was notorious for the foul smells associated with the local leather tanning industry. New market buildings for the buying and selling of hides were constructed in 1879.

Billingsgate Fish Market, Lower Thames Street
Famous for the foul language of its fishmongers and market porters, Billingsgate was rebuilt in 1877 to designs of City of London architect Horace Jones.

Borough Market, Southwark
An ancient fruit and vegetable market, which was rebuilt under the railway arches at London Bridge in 1851. Its food stalls on Friday and Saturday mornings are now a popular tourist attraction.

Brick Lane and Sclater Street, Whitechapel
These were East End street markets for the poorest of the poor. In the 1890s Sclater Street was home to bird-sellers – keeping or breeding the likes of linnets, canaries, chaffinches, bullfinches and starlings was an East End pastime.

Clare Market, nr Aldwych
A small market street, notorious for its unsavoury butcher shops and slaughterhouses. Cleared during the creation of Aldwych and Kingsway in the early 1900s, it is now the site of the London School of Economics

Columbia Market, Bethnal Green
A vast ornate Gothic edifice, erected in 1869 with funds from Angela Burdett-Coutts. However, the local coster-mongers, whom she hoped would relocate to the building, preferred to remain on the streets. It closed as a market in 1874, and was demolished in 1958.

Covent Garden Market
The capital's most famous fruit, vegetable and flower market. It was relocated to a modern site at Nine Elms in 1974. The original market buildings, dating from 1831, now contain shops, restaurants and bars.

Hungerford Market, Charing Cross
A meat, fish, fruit and vegetable market rebuilt by Charles Fowler, architect of Covent Garden Market, in 1833. Demolished in 1860, it was replaced by Charing Cross Railway Station.

Leadenhall Market, Gracechurch Street
Although it also sold meat, fish, poultry, vegetables, leather and hides, Leadenhall became famous for the quality of its poultry and game. It was rebuilt in 1881 by architect Horace Jones.

Metropolitan Cattle Market, Copenhagen Fields
Opened in 1855 in North London to replace the live-stock market at Smithfield. The market's clock tower remains and the grounds are now playing fields.

New Cut, Lambeth
A massive street market for all sorts of food and goods, which was described at length by Henry Mayhew in *London Labour and the London Poor*.

Petticoat Lane, Aldgate
An East End market principally for second-hand clothing. It was run largely by the district's population of Jewish immigrants.

Smithfield Market, Farringdon
This, the capital's ancient livestock market, was rebuilt in the 1850s and 1860s to plans by Horace Jones. It reopened in 1868 as a meat market and is still thriving.

Spitalfields Market, Liverpool Street
A food and vegetable market that was relocated to Leyton, east London in 1991. Its Victorian market buildings, however, have been the subject of a long-running debate over redevelopment.

---

means for a growing store to expand, he added a Foreign Department for the Japanese goods that had become fashionable. Whiteley then expanded into areas such as cleaning and dying (1874) and hair-dressing (1876), then, also in 1876, caused uproar among local shops by introducing food stuffs.

Whiteley dubbed his store 'The Universal Provider', which by the 1880s offered delivery of goods within a twenty-five-mile radius and employed six thousand staff.

The first purpose-built large department store was also in a burgeoning suburb: the Bon Marché opened in 1877 in Brixton, south London. Interestingly, Brixton also went on to claim another shopping first when Electric Avenue opened in 1888 as the first shopping street to be illuminated by electric light.

A New Breed of Consumer
Department stores like Whiteleys and the Bon Marché were innovators, not only in their size and the range of goods on offer under one roof, but in sales techniques. Goods were clearly marked with their prices, and sales were based on cash, rather than the traditional method of an account that was settled annually by the customer, as used by the small businessman.

As department stores increased in size they offered more and more facilities to lure in a new breed of customer – middle-class women who previously might have given their custom to small local traders, but were now emboldened to try the likes of Whiteleys or John Lewis. These stores included cafés and restaurants, lavatories and reading rooms, and turned shops into somewhere more than just places to buy goods.

Above: In the new department stores the Victorian middle classes received personal attention and an unhurried service.

In fact, Whiteleys Refreshment Room, which opened in 1872, was later closed by magistrates on the grounds that it might become a 'place of assignation' – a haunt for adulterers and prostitutes – since there remained a strong whiff of suspicion about any public space in which women had freedom to roam unaccompanied, especially if alcohol was on sale.

All the same, cafés and the like became the norm over the next couple of decades. Indeed, for all local magistrates might worry about public morals, it was ordinary middle-class women who patronized the early department stores, for the goods were generally very reasonably priced and suited the middle-class purse. 'Co-operative' department stores, such as the Army and Navy in Victoria Street, Westminster, which was founded 1871, were brought into being by members of the middle classes clubbing together to buy goods at a discount. In the case of the Army and Navy, it was members of the military and their families; one had to be either a shareholder or buy an annual ticket to shop in the store.

The poor, of course, would not be allowed through the doors of any department store. Equally, the aristocracy preferred the traditional and more exclusive purlieus of Bond Street and St James's, where their families had had accounts for decades.

It is perhaps worth noting, however, that the department store of the 1870s was not a complete

revelation to the Victorian shopper, though it was undoubtedly a novelty. Two forms of 'shopping centre', to use a modern term, already existed in London, in which one might select from a wide range of goods under one roof: the arcade and the bazaar.

ARCADES AND BAZAARS

Of these agreeable semi-promenades, semi-depôts, the most aristocratic is the Burlington Arcade, *Piccadilly. Its shops are chiefly patronised by the wealthier classes, and deal in knick-knackery and hosiery, walking canes, and Paris gants, rather than in the "utilities" which distinguish the glittering "stores" of its plebeian sister, the* Lowther Arcade, *Strand. The latter, to the uninitiated stranger, will probably appear a perfect labyrinth of "toys," through which it would be an Herculean feat to pass uninjuring or uninjured. But the "passage" is accomplished by thousands daily, much to the edification of juvenile Rothschilds, who find here an arena worthy of their abilities.*

CRUCHLEY'S LONDON IN 1865: *A HANDBOOK FOR STRANGERS*, 1865

The nineteenth-century arcade and bazaar both prefigure not only the department store, but also the modern shopping centre.

Arcadia

The arcade was a Regency idea: in essence, it was an elegant pedestrianized covered avenue of individual shops. The first in London was the Opera Arcade, which opened in 1818 behind the Haymarket Opera House (now the Haymarket Theatre). This somewhat gloomy arcade, with shops only on one side, never really took off as a shopping destination. *Punch*, in 1842, described it as 'chiefly resorted to during showers by the temporary houseless, and by those who are caught in the rain while labouring under utter destitution of umbrella or Mackintosh'. Indeed, it gives a similar impression if one visits it today.

The most famous, the Burlington Arcade, which was established in 1819, was always more prosperous, perhaps the result of its superior design and its good location on Piccadilly, a stone's throw from Bond Street. It is well worth a visit today for its nineteenth-century atmosphere. Other arcades followed: the Lowther Arcade in 1830 on the Strand, which was taken over by toy shops before being demolished in 1904; the Exeter Arcade in Wellington Street in the 1850s; the Royal Arcade between Albermarle Street and Bond Street in the 1880s; and the Prince's Arcade between Piccadilly and Jermyn Street also in the 1880s.

Something for Everyone

London's bazaars, on the other hand, were essentially permanent covered markets for the well-to-do. Sadly, none of them survive. As with the arcades, they often featured a range of items for sale and, like the arcades, they were exclusive, guarded by a 'beadle' at the entrance, rather like the modern 'security guard', in order to keep out street urchins and any other undesirable elements.

The two-storey Soho Bazaar in Soho Square flourished from c. 1815 until 1885. It contained various rooms devoted to the 'requirements of ladies and children' – in other words, ornaments and trinkets, millinery, lace, gloves and jewellery – on stalls or open counters ranged on both sides of aisles or passages. The stalls were rented for several shillings a day by between two hundred and four hundred saleswomen, and the bazaar was considered a 'fashionable lounge' for men with time on their hands and an eye for female beauty.

Further down Oxford Street, but still east of Oxford Circus, on the site of the present Marks and Spencer's building, was the Pantheon. In fact, the modern department store has 'Pantheon' on the front, a requirement of the deeds to the site. The Pantheon was similar to the Soho Bazaar, except for a picture

Above: Well-to-do Victorians would have sauntered along Burlington Arcade – which opened in 1819, the year in which Victoria was born – admiring its fashionable stores.

gallery on its upper level. A converted entertainment venue and theatre, it functioned as a bazaar from 1834 until 1867, when it was sold to a wine merchants.

Other bazaars included the Pantechnicon near Belgrave Square, which sold carriages, pianos and furniture (in addition to providing storage for the same), and the Baker Street Bazaar, which dealt in similar items but also housed Madame Tussaud's Wax Works.

Interestingly, as with the first department stores, the arcades and bazaars that preceded them were seen as potentially rather disreputable environments. The saleswomen of the Soho and Pantheon bazaars were doubtless subject to a good deal of male attention, and Burlington Arcade was notoriously a good place to meet prostitutes.

Above: Livestock was frequently driven through the streets of the metropolis on the way to Smithfield Market.

Below: The slum of St Giles, photographed here in 1877, was well known for its second-hand clothes shops.

MARKETS AND MARINE STORES

The butchers of Squalors' Market… are, dear reader, by no means quiet, well-behaved creatures, such as you are acquainted with. Your butcher wears a hat, generally a genteel hat, and a blue coat, and a respectable apron; perhaps, even snowy sleeves and shiny boots, and a nice bit of linen collar above his neckerchief. You give your orders and he receives them decorously, and wishes you good morning as you quit his neatly-arranged and sawdusted shop. Contrasted with him the butcher of Squalors' Market is a mad-man—a raving lunatic. He unscrews the burners of his gaspipes, and creates great spouts of flame that roar and waver in the wind in front of his shamble-like premises… far out from his shop, and attached to roasting-jacks, revolve monstrous pigs' heads and big joints of yellow veal, spiked all over like a porcupine with figure-bearing tickets, that announce the few pence per pound for which the meat may be bought.

JAMES GREENWOOD, *UNSENTIMENTAL JOURNEYS*, 1867

The grand shops, arcades and bazaars of the West End were exclusively for the middle class and the rich. The poor and the working class had a very different shopping experience. Food is a good example. For the wealthy, there were grocers, butchers and bakers of varying quality who each had their own clientèle. Any decent shop delivered goods, on account, to the home. For the lower classes, on the other hand, food purchases were made in street markets or shoddy 'shops' on the edges of the markets.

Of course, London's large wholesale markets were the most famous markets in the capital. These included Smithfield for meat; Billingsgate for fish; Leadenhall for poultry and game; and Covent Garden for fruit and vegetables. Smithfield was a notorious public nuisance, since it also dealt in livestock until the mid-1850s, which meant large herds of cattle were regularly driven through London's most crowded streets. In 1855 the live cattle market was relocated to Copenhagen Fields, north of King's Cross.

In the meantime, grander market buildings were built at Smithfield, which re-opened in 1868 and still flourishes as a meat market. Billingsgate and Leadenhall were also improved and rebuilt in this period, with new buildings opening in 1877 and 1881 respectively. Covent Garden's buildings were also extended, with the Floral Hall in 1860, which is now part of the Royal Opera House, and the Flower Market in 1871, which is now the London Theatre and Transport museums.

Below: Covent Garden's piazza was rebuilt between 1828 and 1831 to the designs of Charles Fowler. The iron and glass roof was added in the 1870s.

Street Markets

Local food markets were less impressive than the likes of Covent Garden or Leadenhall, and were the haunt of poor costermongers and peripatetic street-sellers. Often cheap butcher shops were also nearby. Clare Market, for instance, was a typical example: a small market street, near to Lincoln's Inn, that had a local trade in fruit and vegetables and contained a number of butcher shops. Concerning the goods of the latter, Charles Dickens Jr commented, 'It is meat, and you take it on faith that it is meat of the ox or sheep; but beyond that you can say nothing.' Like most food markets, Clare Market did its best business on a Saturday night, when working men surrendered some proportion of their weekly pay to their wives.

When it came to buying other necessities, the poor could only afford to purchase second-hand goods. In consequence, to take clothing as an example, whole

streets were devoted to the sale of second-hand clothes, garments that were artfully repaired time and again. One such street was Monmouth Street in the St Giles slum, immortalized in Charles Dickens's *Sketches by Boz*. Equally, the shout of 'ol' clo'' was a common street cry, heralding the approach of an old-clothes man. Indeed, virtually anything that could be lifted up, carried or carted was sold by the Victorian capital's itinerant street-sellers.

The Poor's 'Universal Provider'

As for furniture and household goods, there were 'marine stores' – originally stores that supplied goods for ship voyages. The term came to be used for what were little more than shoddy rag and bone dealers, selling anything from battered furniture to second-hand pocket-handkerchiefs.

Pawnbrokers, likewise, where one could browse a range of second-hand items or obtain cash in a hurry, were also a feature of most slum areas. This was as near as many Londoners got to a 'Universal Provider', but one doubts that the service in such establishments, whose counters were divided by thin wooden panels to create private booths, was quite that received by customers at William Whiteley's.

Below: Fly-posting, both on legitimate hoardings and otherwise, was a lucrative business.

ADVERTISING

It is said that everything is to be had in London. There is truth enough in the observation; indeed, rather too much. The conviction that everything is to be had, whether you are in want of it or not, is forced upon you with a persistence that becomes oppressive; and you find that, owing to everything being so abundantly plentiful, there is one thing which is not to be had, do what you will, though you would like to have it if you could – and that one thing is just one day's exemption from the persecutions of Puff in its myriad shapes and disguises.

CHARLES MANBY SMITH, *CURIOSITIES OF LONDON LIFE*, 1853

William Whiteley never took out advertising for his famous department store, relying instead on it being newsworthy enough to get repeated mentions in the local press. As the century progressed, however, he proved to be an exception.

The 'Ad-man' Cometh

Many Victorian commentators on London complained of being swamped by advertising. There were handbills fly-posted on every available surface, sandwich-board men and even slow-moving vans made up to resemble giant exemplars of the product advertised, such as coaches mocked up as giant hats. It was often hard to escape the 'polite request' or 'hint' or 'beg to inform' – such was the polite but insistent language of the Victorian advertiser – directing you to particular shops and products.

Equally, gas, and later electricity, was being used to illuminate shop windows to an unprecedented degree. Giant letters began to appear on buildings, spelling out 'Bovril' or some other mass-market product. More and more advertisements seemed to appear at the beginning and end of books. Max Schlesinger, a German visiting London in the 1850s, remarked on the omnipresence of advertisements 'on the steam-boat wharf, and under the water in the Thames tunnel… on the highest chimneys… in coloured letters on street lamps… the prologue of all the newspapers, and the epilogue of all the books… in the railway carriages… on the paddle-boxes of the steamers.'

Interestingly, the same techniques used today were also used in the nineteenth century. Take, for example, the Patent 'Vowel' Washing Machine, advertised in 1879 with endorsements such as, 'My servants wash more clothes and much better in one day with your Machine than they used to do in

three days without it.' Servants may no longer be available, but washing products are still sold using similar sentiments. Nevertheless, the Victorians, far from being naïve about their booming 'consumer culture', found the cliché and repetition of adverts just as annoying as we do. Why, for instance, asked *Punch* in 1842, must every product be the *original* so-and-so, or every firm be *general* in its services, as in 'Nunhead Cemetery is now open for *general* interment'? But *Punch* provided no answer, and cartoons critical of advertising, satirizing peculiar or grandiose advertisements, would appear in the journal, but went unheeded by shops and salesmen throughout the century.

Below: Ludgate Circus at the turn of the century was a popular spot for large advertisements; note the two famous Victorian brands: Bovril's meat extract and Vinolia soap.

Above: Companies, such as Cadbury's (founded in Birmingham in 1824), became increasingly sophisticated in their use of advertising during the Victorian era.

TRANSPORT

ON FOOT

Strangers in London are not fond of walking, they are bewildered by the crowd, and frightened at the crossings; they complain of the brutal conduct of the English, who elbow their way along the pavement without considering that people who hurry on, on some important business or other, cannot possibly stop to discuss each kick or push they give or receive. A Londoner jostles you in the street, without ever dreaming of asking your pardon… None but men of business care to walk through the City at business hours; but if, either from choice or necessity, you find your way into those crowded quarters, you had better walk with your eyes wide open. Don't stop on the pavement, move on as fast you can, and do as the others do, that is to say, struggle on as best you may, and push forward without any false modesty. The passengers in London streets are hardened… You have not been introduced to them; you are a stranger to them, and there is no reason why they should consult your convenience.

MAX SCHLESINGER, *SAUNTERINGS IN LONDON*, 1853

Max Schlesinger found the typical Londoner to be less than gracious to his fellow pedestrians. Yet, like many others who came to London, he was impressed by the sheer bustle of the capital's streets, and the vast numbers of people who thronged its pavements.

Much of this 'human tide' was on foot out of sheer necessity, since the average worker could not afford any other means of transport. Omnibuses in the 1850s were prohibitively expensive for the working class; as were the railways until the increasing availability of 'workmen's fares' – cheap fares at morning and evening rush hour – in the second half of the century, particularly after the Cheap Trains Act of 1883.

Cost, however, was not the only factor. Most Londoners were simply accustomed to walking long distances. It was not uncommon for city clerks living in suburbs such as Islington and Holloway, who could afford the omnibus, to prefer the exercise of walking several miles to and from work. Admittedly, walking undoubtedly declined as transport became cheaper. By the 1880s, *Cassell's Household Guide* was advising that 'business gentlemen and young people' might do well to form the habit of walking to and from 'office, warehouse, or school', and become 'healthier and

Above: *Fleet Street was notorious for heavy horse-drawn traffic, while in the middle distance a bridge carries the London, Chatham and Dover Railway over Ludgate Hill.*

Opposite: *Tower Bridge opened in 1894 to provide a much-needed river crossing in east London. Its towers conceal the hydraulics and counterweights that allow the central spans to pivot open for tall ships.*

stronger in nerve and physique' (note that ladies were not expected to walk the streets), rather than take the train. Nonetheless, even as more people used public transport, walking several miles into London to one's place of work was not considered remarkable.

A Hazardous Journey

The streets themselves were not always easy to navigate. Though it now has a rather clichéd association with the Victorian capital, fog was often a major problem in winter, causing traffic accidents and making long journeys untenable, because of both restricted vision and the poisonous atmosphere, resulting from soot trapped in the damp air. In fact,

London fogs were described by American writer Nathaniel Hawthorne as 'a distillation of mud'; commonly known as 'pea-soupers', they could range in colour from a yellow, orange or brown tinge to utterly black; such was the degree of pollution caused by coal fires and factory chimneys.

There were other hazards, too. In particular, the Victorians were as familiar with 'road works' as we are today. The writer George Sala, for instance, complained in 1859 of blocked streets caused by the 'incessant paving, lighting, sewerage, or electric telegraph communications of underground London'.

The state of pavements and road surfaces were a long-standing problem in London. Until 1855, when a single Metropolitan Board of Works was created, they had been inconsistently maintained or, in many cases, neglected by a plethora of independent local bodies. Furthermore, while in the West End both wooden and stone pavements were a common feature, many poor outlying districts were not paved at all. In central areas where roads were surfaced – the West End and the City – the preference was generally for a layer of granite, known as 'macadam', although asphalt made some progress from the 1870s. Macadam consisted of equal-sized small pieces of granite packed close together and ground into a smooth surface by the passage of traffic. The macadamized roads required regular repair and chunks of granite would frequently come loose, either due to bad laying of the material or simple wear and tear, creating pot-holes that quickly filled with mud.

Mud, dust and dirt coated London's roads. Much of the debris was undoubtedly horse-dung, and coal fires contributed a fine layer of filth that settled everywhere. In slum areas, all sorts of household refuse would be dumped upon the streets. In consequence, all decent houses had iron boot-scrapers on their doorsteps for removing the worst of the filth, while in the streets crossing-sweepers – often poor or homeless children – worked with brooms to clear a path from one side of the road to the other, for anyone who looked likely to provide a tip.

Above: A female crossing-sweeper begs a disinterested pedestrian for change. Crossing-sweepers performed a useful function in London's muddy streets.

The final recourse for ladies, of whom decency required skirts down to their ankles, was simply to wear a pair of stout boots and have a very agile step. In 1852, an American writer called David Bartlett noted, for instance, that 'An American town-bred lady would as soon think of swimming up the Thames against tide, as walking far in such ankle-deep mud, but English ladies do it, and with consummate dexterity too.'

HORSE-DRAWN TRAFFIC

ELEVEN A.M. One of the wheelers of a four-horse omnibus slipped on the pavement and fell down at the foot of the Holborn-side obelisk, between Fleet-street and Ludgate-hill. There's a stoppage. The horse makes vain endeavours to get up; there is no help for it, they must undo reins, buckles and straps to free him. But a stoppage of five minutes in Fleet-street creates a stoppage in every direction to the distance of perhaps half a mile or a mile... this vast space presents the curious spectacle of scores of omnibuses, cabs, gigs, horses, carts, brewer's drays, coal waggons, all standing still, and jammed into an inextricable fix. Some madcap of a boy attempts the perilous passage from one side of the street to the other; he jumps over carts, creeps under the bellies of horses, and, in spite of the manifold dangers which beset him, he gains the opposite pavement. But those who can spare the time or who set some store by their lives, had better wait.

MAX SCHLESINGER, *SAUNTERINGS IN LONDON*, 1853

The traffic jam was a perennial feature of life in Victorian London, just as it is today; and the cause was not necessarily just road works. Accidents were also common, as horses often stumbled on mud, ice or simply an uneven surface, and had difficulty raising themselves.

Sometimes, however, the obstruction was exacerbated by the old and narrow streets of the capital. The Victorians knew this full well and went some way to addressing the problem, with many obstructions and nuisances gradually removed during the nineteenth century.

The horse and cattle market at Smithfield, which regularly caused chaos as animals were driven through the streets of central London, was moved to Islington in 1855. The ancient, arched monument of Temple Bar, which marked the border between the City of London and Westminster and was notorious for causing congestion, was pulled down in 1878 to facilitate traffic along Fleet Street. The arch was relocated to a country estate outside the capital, but there are now plans to re-erect it near St Paul's Cathedral.

Moreover, during the 1860s and 1870s, the old toll-gates of the previous century, whether on roads or bridges over the Thames, were all removed, freeing up not only vehicular but pedestrian traffic. Many workers living in south London, for instance, avoided Waterloo Bridge and used toll-free Westminster or Blackfriars bridges. And, of course, new roads were constructed: New Oxford Street was opened in 1847,

Queen Victoria Street in 1871, Northumberland Avenue in 1874, Shaftesbury Avenue in 1886 and Charing Cross Road in 1887.

Bridging the Thames

Further progress in reducing the congestion in central London involved the construction or reconstruction of several bridges over the Thames. These included the Hungerford Suspension Bridge in 1845, which was replaced by a rail and foot bridge in 1864; Chelsea Bridge in 1858; Lambeth Bridge in 1862; and the Gothic masterpiece of Tower Bridge in 1894. Meanwhile, the great engineering work of Holborn Viaduct, crossing the steep valley on either side of Farringdon Road, was finished in 1869.

Furthermore, various embankments were built along the Thames where, previously, narrow sets of steps had descended down to wooden wharves and a muddy shoreline. Admittedly, the embankments were not designed merely to improve traffic flow.

Below: Westminster Bridge first opened in 1750, but was rebuilt in 1854–62 by Thomas Page, with Charles Barry, architect of the Houses of Parliament, acting as a consultant.

Above: Waterloo Bridge was freed from tolls in 1877. Note the factories and breweries, now all gone, that once lined the south bank of the River Thames.

The Albert and Chelsea embankments, completed in 1869 and 1874 respectively, were designed primarily to guard against flooding. The Victoria Embankment, running between Blackfriars Bridge and Westminster opened in 1870, was a brilliant multi-purpose piece of engineering. Underneath the road was a tunnel for the latest underground railway

Below: Sir Joseph Bazalgette's engineering masterpiece, Victoria Embankment, under construction in the 1860s.

(now the Circle and District Line), pipes for water and gas and, of course, a section of Joseph's Bazalgette's new system of sewers. It was also an alternative road for anyone wishing to eschew the congestion of Fleet Street and the Strand.

In fact, the Victorians remodelled a good deal of the metropolitan road network. The final great road-building scheme of the era was the construction of Aldwych and Kingsway, major thoroughfares that linked the Strand to Holborn. Work, however, did not get under way until 1900, and the project was only finished in 1905.

Public Transport

Who used the capital's roads? At the start of the nineteenth century, the only public transport available was the cab. Four-wheeled cabs included not only custom-made vehicles, but 'hackney coaches' or 'growlers' – second-hand coaches, formerly in private hands and often in poor condition. In the early years of Victoria's reign, the two-seater hansom cab was introduced, with its distinctive two large wheels, and driver perched on top at the rear. It proved popular, being faster and more manoeuvrable than its predecessors, and by the 1870s fifty per cent of the cabs in London were hansoms as opposed to the Clarence (four-wheeled) variety. But cabs suffered from a reputation for overcharging, despite being licensed, and disputes over fares and distance travelled were common throughout the century.

In 1829, however, an alternative to the cab appeared, which revolutionized transport in London – the omnibus.

Above: *Holborn Viaduct, which bridges Farringdon Road, was a vast undertaking that was eventually completed in 1869. The viaduct is ornamented by four statues dedicated to 'Commerce', 'Agriculture', 'Fine Arts' and 'Science'.*

OMNIBUS AND TRAM

Never ride inside an omnibus—I apostrophise, of course, the men folks... the vehicular ascent is incommodious, not to say indecorous, for the fair sex. But Ho, ye men, don't ride inside. A friend of mine had once his tibia fractured by the diagonal brass rod that crosses the door; the door itself being violently slammed to, as is the usual custom, by the conductor. Another of my acquaintance was pitched head foremost from the interior, on the mockingly fallacious cry of 'all right' being given... Inside an omnibus you are subjected to innumerable vexations and annoyances. Sticks or parasols are poked in your chest... you are half suffocated by the steam of damp umbrellas; your toes are crushed to atoms as the passengers alight or ascend; you are very probably the next neighbour to persons suffering under vexatious ailments, such as asthma, simple cold in the head, or St. Vitus's dance; it is ten to one but that you suffer under the plague of babies; and, five days out of the seven, you will have a pickpocket, male or female, for a fellow-passenger.

GEORGE SALA, *TWICE ROUND THE CLOCK*, 1859

The omnibus was introduced to London by a Mr Shillibeer in 1829, on a route from Paddington to the Bank of England. The buses were large coaches that could carry up to twenty people inside, albeit in very cramped conditions. Bus stops did not exist and, consequently until bells were introduced, both alighting and exiting one of the new buses required the passenger to somehow catch the attention of the

FROM A BAROUCHE TO A BROUGHAM

There were many private vehicles belonging to the middle and upper classes. These varied in size, cost and speed, just as cars do today. Carriages, on the whole, were expensive to buy and run. Many, therefore, were hired, along with the requisite horses and coachmen. The wealthy in particular would often rent a vehicle for the London season, to spare themselves the trouble of transporting their country carriages into town. The hired carriage could be kept in the family's own mews or in a nearby livery stable. The middle classes, on the other hand, were more likely to hire a carriage for a day-trip to impress their friends and neighbours.

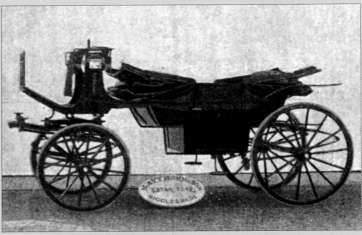

Landau carriages featured convertible hoods.

Landau
A grand four-seater, four-wheel carriage in which passengers were seated face to face – two facing forwards and two facing back. Driven by a coachman on a box seat at the front, with four horses, it was a convertible – its roof was a hood of two parts, of which the rear could be folded back and the front could be folded or removed.

Sociable
A four-person open carriage, similar to a landau; also driven by a coachman, but with two horses.

Barouche
This carriage differed from the landau in that only the rear passengers could be covered by a folding hood.

Brougham
The typical carriage of the Victorian middle classes. A smaller, enclosed four-wheel carriage, generally seating only two. Also driven by a coachman (again, on a box seat at the front), with a single horse. It was more economical than the carriages listed above, yet still stylish enough to impress the neighbours.

Hansom cabs were the Victorian equivalent of our black cabs.

Victoria
Popular with ladies, this was a small two-seater, four-wheel carriage with a collapsible hood. It was driven by a coachman and generally just one horse, and featured curved open sides protected by mud guards rather than doors, thus allowing easy access to women wearing voluminous skirts.

Phaeton
A sporty, lightweight, four-wheel (one- or two-horse) open carriage for one or two passengers. It was low-built with no doors, like the Victoria. One passenger would also drive the vehicle, rather than a coachman.

Dog-cart
A two-wheeled open carriage in which driver and passenger sat back-to-back. Thus named because originally this type of vehicle was used to transport sportsmen's dogs, either in a box under the driver's seat or by enclosing the rear seat.

Curricle
A sporty, hooded, two-wheeler, drawn by two horses; popular in the early part of the nineteenth century.

Cabriolet
An economical replacement for the curricle; a hooded, two-wheeled light carriage, but drawn by a single horse.

Gig
A generic term ('trap' was also used) for a light two-wheeled, one- or two-seater carriage, open or hooded, and drawn by a single horse. The Stanhope was a one-seater gig and the Tilbury was a two-seater.

Fly
A one-horse covered carriage, which was often used as a station cab in country districts.

driver. This new method of transport, which was soon abbreviated to 'bus', proved popular and routes began to appear all over London.

Originally, Shillibeer's buses were kept out of the centre of the metropolis by the monopoly granted to hackney coaches, but this was lifted in 1832, and the only restriction on routes was the expense of passing through turnpikes. Thus, many suburban routes terminated just short of turnpike gates, often making old coaching inns, such as the Angel, Islington, de facto bus termini.

Top Deck

By the 1850s, 'knifeboard' double-decker buses had been introduced, in effect doubling the number of passengers that might be carried. Gentlemen ascended a ladder to the open top deck, and sat back-to-back on a narrow bench (the 'knifeboard'). George Sala considered such clambering about as 'incommodious, not to say indecorous' for women, and the top deck was strictly a male domain. In wet weather, men travelling inside the bus were frequently asked to 'oblige a lady' by surrendering their seat and leaving to sit on top in the rain. In some cases, the impression one gets is that this was done rather grudgingly: a parody in *Punch* has an 'Old Bachelor' complain 'I should like to see a lady ever doing the same for a gentleman!'.

By the end of the century, the interior and exterior of buses had considerably improved – winding stairs ascended to the top deck where 'garden seats', facing forwards (unlike the 'knifeboard') were the norm; and women were free to sit on the top deck if they wished.

Horse-drawn trams did not appear until the 1860s, and only began to flourish in the 1870s and 1880s, as an ever-increasing network of tracks were laid. They were, however, principally suburban and not intro-duced into the crowded streets of the West End or the City, with trams from

Above: Two-wheeled hansom cabs had greater mobility and speed than their four-wheeled predecessors. The cab's number was always clearly displayed, in case of disputes over fares.
Below: In this 1876 Punch cartoon, 'Chivalry in the London Streets', the gentlemen push ladies aside, fighting to get onto an omnibus and out of the driving rain.

Left: Pedestrians walk briskly to catch up with a 'garden-seat' omnibus, which allowed passengers to sit facing forward. Omnibuses were often covered with adverts.

Opposite: Bicycling became fashionable during the 1890s. Women's dress was a problem, however, because of their voluminous skirts, and prudish Victorians objected to 'bloomer'-style trousers or a split skirt as 'unwomanly'.

the south terminating at the various bridges along the Thames: those from the west at Shepherd's Bush and Hammersmith; from the north at Euston and King's Cross; and from the east at Moorgate and Aldgate.

AUTOMOBILITY

One of the most entertaining features of this revived interest in what it is the fashion to call automobility, is the series of laments as to the supersession of the horse... The railways also were to have wiped out the horses, but have they? There are more horses now than there ever were.

THE LEISURE HOUR, 1896

Again, there is no 'loving' of a reservoir; you must feed it, indeed, but it does not care to be patted. You can't give it a carrot or lump of sugar before you start. Perhaps some ingenious inventor will enable a motor to neigh instead of 'toot,' but it can never become an affectionate companion who knows your voice and likes to be stroked. There is bloodless satisfaction in steering the best horseless carriage, however swiftly and safely it may carry you where you would go.

Perhaps it is in the application of the new motive power to bicycles that we shall see it most enjoyably appreciated...

THE LEISURE HOUR, 1896

If the first revolution in London's road transport occurred just before the Victorian era with the omnibus, another occurred at the end of Victoria's reign, in the 1890s, with two novel vehicles increasingly seen in London – the bicycle and the motor car.

Two Wheels or Four?

In fairness, the bicycle was not actually new. Earlier in the century it was known as the 'velocipede', and arguably the bicycle was invented in the eighteenth century. Bicycle races were held in London in the 1870s. However, it was the invention of the 'safety bicycle' and pneumatic tyre in the 1880s that allowed women to buy bikes, and, in some cases, gave them freedom to travel at will, unchaperoned.

This resulted in a 'bicycle craze' in the 1890s, with the elegant, wealthy lady bicyclists who congregated in Battersea Park being one of the sights of the 1895 Season. Cyclists were at first excluded from Hyde Park – hence the fashion to visit Battersea. Cycling songs like *Daisy Bell* ('But you'll look sweet, Upon the seat, Of a bicycle made for two!') became popular in the music hall, and the bloomer-style cycling dress for women was, naturally, the object of fun in *Punch* and elsewhere.

The car, on the other hand, was not so fashionable and did not have a chance to have much impact before the end of Victoria's reign, but a few examples of the 'auto-motor' appeared on the capital's streets from 1896, together with motor-buses from 1897. The automobile was not necessarily expected to replace the horse. It was, traditionalists claimed, rather unpredictable in its movements, making crossing the road even more hazardous than previously. How would people manage without the intelligence of horses, which could actively avoid obstacles in the street?

Traffic lights, of course, did not exist; a gas-powered light attempted in 1868 had exploded within a year and the experiment was not continued. What new class of 'coachmen' would have to be trained to drive the vehicles? Needless to say, it did not take many years for these questions to be answered, as horse-drawn traffic all but disappeared from London streets within the space of a generation.

RAILWAYS

Punctuality may be the soul of business, but suppose not that it is the spirit of railways. If you do not care whether you keep an appointment or not, make it on the faith of the Company, by all means; but otherwise by none. Regard starting, or arriving at your destination, only half an hour too late, as luck. You pay nothing extra to attendants for civility, so you must not hope for it.

PUNCH, 1844

The quintessential Victorian innovation in transport was, of course, the train. Interestingly, the Victorian railway was not the model of efficiency that we nostalgically might imagine, or at least, not in the early years, but the progress of steam in London was unstoppable. It began with a short line from London Bridge to Greenwich that opened in 1836, and then the impressive Euston Station opened in 1837 to serve the London to Birmingham railway. The

Right: The clock at King's Cross Station was originally displayed at the Great Exhibition of 1851 and later placed in the clock tower of the station for its opening in 1852.

station's exterior originally included a vast monumental arch, which was sadly demolished in 1962.

Station to Station

Gradually, a succession of stations was developed on the periphery of central London by various train companies, amounting to a dozen or so major lines and stations by the 1880s, most of which are still in use today. These were Paddington in 1838; Fenchurch Street in 1841; Waterloo in 1848; King's Cross in 1852; Victoria in 1860; Cannon Street in 1866; St Pancras in 1868; Liverpool Street in 1874; and

Below: The first station at Paddington opened in 1838 with wooden buildings. A more permanent replacement, designed by Isambard Kingdom Brunel, was completed in 1854.

Blackfriars in 1886. Local and suburban branch lines also flourished, promoting, along with the omnibus and tram lines, the growth of commuter suburbs.

And yet, although the railways enabled a new era of high-speed travel, there was a negative side. Firstly, a good deal of land was needed to build stations and tracks; much of this was provided by slum clearances, such as the demolition of Agar Town, which was replaced by St Pancras Station. Such clearances had a knock-on effect on overcrowding elsewhere in the city. And, even if one applauded the removal of slum housing, albeit with no effort to re-house those living there, railway developments were quite capable of blighting an area themselves.

True, the stations were often built to impress, the Gothic masterpiece of St Pancras being the best

example. An article in *The Builder* in 1875 famously stated that 'Railway termini and hotels are to the nineteenth century what monasteries and cathedrals were to the thirteenth century.' But what of the rails, bridges, tunnels and tracks? The London and Dover Railway, for instance, obscured the view of St Paul's Cathedral from Ludgate Hill with an ugly viaduct built in the 1860s. And what of the effect on the environment? One can only imagine the incessant noise, dirt and smoke inflicted on those living in the houses adjoining the railway arches and viaducts around London Bridge and The Borough.

End of an Era
The greatest losers in the railway boom were those associated with the business of coaching, previously the only means of 'inter-city' travel. The stage coaches of the previous generation – four passengers inside, eight outside – not only employed drivers and inn-keepers en route between towns, but there were vast coaching inns in the metropolis, the largest of which – for example, the Bull and Mouth on St Martin's-le-Grand in the City – could stable several hundred horses. Following the advent of the railways, the inns went out of business one by one. Admittedly, the effect was not instantaneous; indeed, it took a generation, but the disappearance of the coaching inns marked the end of an era and presaged the end of horse-drawn traffic.

Below: The Charing Cross Station and Hotel was erected in 1863–4. The Charing Cross monument in the forecourt also dates from 1863 and is a replica of the medieval original.

Above: The glorious Midland Grand Hotel at St Pancras Station was designed by George Gilbert Scott and opened in 1873, five years after the completion of the railway station.

UNDERGROUND

The Metropolitan Railway... opened to the public on the 10th inst. and it was calculated that more than 30,000 person were carried over the line in the course of the day. Indeed, the desire to travel by this line on the opening day was more than the directors had provided for; and from nine o'clock *in the morning till past mid-day it was impossible to obtain a place on the up or Cityward line at any of the mid stations. In the evening the tide turned, and the crush at the Farringdon St. station was as great as at the door of a theatre of the first night of some popular performer... Notwithstanding the throng, it is gratifying to add that no accident occurred, and the report of the passengers was unanimous in favour of the smoothness and comfort of the line.*

THE ILLUSTRATED LONDON NEWS, 10 JANUARY 1863

While railways were built to carry Londoners in and out of the city, there were those who recognized their potential as a mode of transport between the different railway termini and through the very heart of the metropolis. To this end, a Select Committee on Metropolitan Communications sat in 1855 and considered various suggestions. These included a 'Crystal Way' – a glass covered arcade with trains beneath it, running between St Paul's and Oxford Circus – and a similar covered arcade design by Joseph Paxton, running between all major termini, but with the trains raised above ground level.

In both cases, it was envisioned the trains would be powered by atmospheric pressure, creating an engineless, smoke-free environment. Neither idea, however, was taken any further, partly because of the immense cost and partly because the atmospheric system was not up to task. London's only atmospheric line, from Forest Hill to Croydon in south London, opened in the 1840s, but it was only a matter of months before it was swiftly converted to steam.

There was, however, a less grandiose plan for an underground link between the City (or, rather its borders, starting at Farringdon Street) and Paddington, via King's Cross, and it was this that was carried forward eventually. Consequently, in 1860, work began on the construction of the Metropolitan Railway, the first underground railway in the world.

Going Underground

Not everyone thought it a good idea. One reason for this was the Thames Tunnel that passed under the river between Wapping and Rotherhithe. Although completed some twenty years earlier in 1843 and acknowledged as a miracle of engineering, the tunnel had taken eighteen years to complete, cost an inordinate amount of money and there had been several deaths during the construction, due to repeated flooding. Moreover, there were insufficient funds to provide ramps for carriages in the tunnel (as had been originally intended) and so it had remained a foot tunnel, making little money for its owners, and acquired something of a seedy reputation as the haunt of hawkers and prostitutes. Even though the Metropolitan Railway did not have to cross the Thames, *The Times* still called the scheme 'Utopian' and classed it with such 'bold but hazardous propositions' as 'flying machines, warfare by balloons' and 'tunnels under the channel'.

In fact, the Metropolitan Railway was actually flooded during its construction by the old Fleet River, which had long since been driven underground and used as part of the city's sewer system. Nevertheless, work continued, and relatively quickly at that. One advantage the builders had was that they were using a 'cut and cover' system – digging cuttings, and then covering over the top – rather than boring deep into the earth. By 1863 the railway opened its stations: Farringdon, King's Cross, Gower Street (now Euston Square), Portland Road (now Great Portland Street), Baker Street, Edgware Road and Paddington. The journey took just over half an hour, and *The Times* recanted, calling it 'the greatest engineering triumph of the day'.

The Dark and the Dirt

The trains on the Metropolitan Line were, like all Victorian trains, divided into first, second and third class. The first-class carriages boasted cushioned seats, the third merely bare wooden benches. Remarkably, they were all lit by gas contained in collapsible bags

Below: Paddington was the terminus of the world's first underground railway, the Metropolitan Railway, which opened in 1863.

and fixed on the roof of the carriages. The bags were periodically refilled with gas at the stations. Oil lamps would later come into use. Unfortunately, despite the best efforts of engineers, there was a good deal of smoke and dirt in the tunnels. The air was reportedly heavy with the smell of sulphur and coal dust, not to mention the aroma of gentlemen smoking their pipes.

Despite such conditions – and it is worth bearing in mind that the atmosphere above ground was often fairly noxious, too – the Metropolitan Railway proved a success and other underground lines followed. During the 1860s, the Metropolitan extended north to Swiss Cottage, south to South Kensington, west to Hammersmith and east to Moorgate. Further progress east came with Liverpool Street in 1875 and Tower Hill in 1882. Meanwhile, the Metropolitan District Railway (forerunner of the District Line) opened in 1868 and, by 1871, ran services between Brompton, Earl's Court, High Street Kensington and the Mansion House through stations that are still in use today. The Circle Line was created when the District Line reached Tower Hill in 1884.

Improving Connections

Other lines included the East London Railway (now the East London Line) between New Cross and Shoreditch, which had taken over the Thames Tunnel and converted it to rail use and opened in 1876; the City and South London Railway, forerunner of the Northern Line, which ran from King William Street in the City of London to Stockwell, opened in 1890 and had reached Angel in the north by 1901; the Waterloo and City line between Bank and Waterloo opened in 1898; and, finally, the Central London Railway (Central Line), which ran from Liverpool Street to Shepherd's Bush, opened in 1900.

Above: Blackfriars acquired an underground station in 1870 to accommodate an extension of the growing Metropolitan District Railway.

Right: St Katherine Dock opened in 1828 and soon became one of London's busiest docks. It is now an exclusive marina for the boats of the rich and famous.

Other new underground ventures were attempted. The Blackwall Tunnel, for road traffic, built 1891–7, is still in use today. It was, however, the third tunnel under the Thames. The second, after the Thames Tunnel, was the now forgotten Tower Subway near the Tower of London, which opened in 1870. Originally, it contained small carriages that were pulled back and forth on a cable system. It attracted few passengers, however, and was swiftly converted to pedestrian use. Even then, it was terribly cramped; Charles Dickens Jr wrote in 1879, 'there is not much head-room… and it is not advisable for any but the very briefest of Her Majesty's lieges to attempt the passage in high-heeled boots, or with a hat to which he attaches any particular value'. Nonetheless, it lasted until 1894, when Tower Bridge was opened. Although unknown to most Londoners, it is still in use housing cabling and pipes for various utilities.

THE SILENT HIGHWAY

… you are not to delude yourself, that either by wheeled vehicle or by the humbler conveyances known as "Shanks's mare," and the "Marrowbone stage"—in more refined language, walking—have all those who have business in the city reached their destination. No; the Silent Highway has been their travelling route… in swift, grimy little steamboats, crowded with living freights from Chelsea, and Pimlico, and Vauxhall piers, from Hungerford, Waterloo, Temple, Blackfriars, and Southwark— straight by the hay-boats,… straight by Thames police hulks, by four and six-oared cutters, by coal-barges, and great lighters laden with bricks and ashes… to the Old Shades Pier, hard by London Bridge.

GEORGE SALA, *TWICE ROUND THE CLOCK*, 1859

Above: Steamboats were used on the River Thames both as commuter ferries and as pleasure boats, travelling as far afield as Margate and the Kent coast.

Opposite: The Victorian warehouses of Wapping High Street, formerly in the heart of London's wharves and docks, now contain luxury loft apartments.

The Thames or 'Silent Highway' was a significant part of the capital's Victorian transport infrastructure. Small passenger steamboats were a common sight on the river by the 1820s, and they continued to offer a swift alternative to rail and road throughout the century for commuters, although their importance declined as the underground railway network developed and as more bridges crossed the Thames.

Larger steamboats travelled further downstream, generally ferrying holidaymakers to pleasure gardens at Rosherville, near Gravesend, and out along the coast to seaside resorts like Margate. It was one such boat, the *Princess Alice*, that sank in the worst disaster on the river during Victoria's reign. Returning from Rosherville on 3 September, 1878, it collided with the *Bywell Castle*, a large collier, and over six hundred lives were lost.

An Ancient Trading Route

The importance of the Thames, however, was in trade. London was the largest port in the world, importing vast amounts of raw materials from Britain's colonies, and exporting, in turn, the country's manufactured goods. Large sailing ships and steamboats constantly plied the river and unloaded their cargoes into the capital's complex system of docks. In fact, the docks themselves were among the tourist sights of Victorian London.

Begun in 1790 with the small Brunswick Dock at Blackwall and then the bigger West India Dock in 1802, the 'Docklands' gradually expanded both westwards to just east of the Tower of London – the building of St Katherine Dock, which opened in 1828, involved demolishing over 1200 houses – south down the Isle of Dogs – Millwall Dock opened

in 1866 – and, most significantly, east to the larger Victoria and Albert Docks, which opened in 1855 and 1880 respectively, and which were designed to cope with the ever-increasing volume of traffic and size of ships.

Docklands

From the outside, the distinctive feature of the docks was their walls – several stories high to provide essential security from pilfering, both by outsiders and those working in the docks – and the forests of masts of ships that poked out above them. Within the walls, however, the visitor could see every kind of product from the four corners of the world being unloaded and stored by the 'lumpers', 'whippers' and 'lightermen' who were employed on a casual basis to carry the back-breaking loads.

The variety of sights and smells were reportedly

Left: London's docks received vessels from all over the world, supporting the import and export of a vast amount of goods.

Below: Sailing ships were gradually replaced by steamers during the Victorian period.

astonishing. The West India Docks, alone had massive warehouses containing sugar, tea, coffee, rum, Madeira, mahogany, logwood, flour, cocoa and spices of all kinds. There were also cavernous subterranean wine vaults at the London Docks: a regular stopping-off point for tourists who enjoyed the free 'samples' on offer.

The dock workers themselves, of course, could not sample the goods, unless they wished to be prosecuted and imprisoned. Yet theft was still a regular occurrence, partly because dockers themselves were treated so badly by their employers, often taken on for merely a few hours at a time and having to fight daily with other men to come to the attention of the hiring foreman.

In 1849, Henry Mayhew described the casual dockers outside the London Docks as 'decayed and bankrupt master butchers, master bakers, publicans, grocers, old soldiers, old sailors, Polish refugees, broken-down gentlemen, discharged lawyers' clerks, suspended Government clerks, almsmen, pensioners, servants, thieves'. For the docks were one of the few places one could get employment without a written reference. It was only in 1889, following a major

strike by London's dockers, that conditions began to improve for the workers who relied on the 'Silent Highway' for their daily bread.

Above: St Katherine Dock once had extensive underground wine vaults, which have since been converted into a car-park.
Below: Millwall Dock, 200 acres of reclaimed marshland, opened in 1868, closing only in 1980 when the area was extensively redeveloped to become the home of big business.

AFTERWORD

Above: Cleopatra's Needle is one of London's oldest monuments, dating from c. 1500 BC. The obelisk was given to Britain after the British Army defeated Napoleon in Egypt in 1819; it was relocated to London in 1877.

It may surprise readers to know that, until a few years ago, I had no interest in Victorian London whatsoever. In fact, my only experience of the capital was occasional half-hearted visits as a student. My typical sojourn in the city involved walking the length of Oxford Street and back again. Anything else seemed far too challenging, especially without the aid of a map.

And yet, when circumstances brought me to live and study in London in 1994, something changed. I began to notice mews, alleys and courts that belonged to a previous era. I recognized street names that I had read in the novels of Charles Dickens as a child. And the more I walked the streets, rather than plunging into the oblivion of the undergound, the more I discovered buildings and places that fascinated and startled me; the old mixed with the new at every turn. I made a resolution to be more curious, to explore the past; and this book is one result of such curiosity.

Of course, Victorian London is a large, daunting subject for any writer. Consequently, although I have tried to cover the aspects of life in London that underwent the most change during the nineteenth century, inevitably much has been neglected due to lack of space. My only aspiration for this book is that it may encourage a few readers to take a more active interest in the Victorian city and to take pleasure in the echoes of Victorian life that still surround us – not least the remarkable buildings, museums and other locations pictured in the preceding chapters.

I would like to leave the last word, however, to one of the greatest Victorian writers on life in London, the journalist Henry Mayhew. Mayhew actually begins his *Letters to the Morning Chronicle*, which document the misery of the metropolitan poor, with a timeless evocation of the splendour of The Great Metropolis. It is a piece of writing that echoes my own thoughts, whenever I return home to this marvellous city:

The noblest prospect in the world, it has been well said, is London viewed from the suburbs on a clear winter's evening. The stars are shining in the heavens, but there is another firmament spread out below, with its millions of bright lights glittering at our feet. Line after line sparkles, like the trails left by meteors, cutting and crossing one another till they are lost in the haze of the distance. Over the whole there hangs a lurid cloud, bright as if the monster city were in flames, and looking afar off like the sea by night, made phosphorescent by the million creatures dwelling within it.

SELECT BIBLIOGRAPHY

Most of the nineteenth-century sources, including various guidebooks, travelogues and pieces of journalism, to which I have referred when writing this book are available in part or in full on my Victorian Dictionary website, **http://www.victorianlondon.org**. They are far too numerous to list here, but if a reader is looking for contemporary descriptions of London life in the nineteenth century I would recommend starting with:

Dickens, Charles Jr, *Dickens's Dictionary of London* (Charles Dickens and Evans, 1879)

Sala, George, *Twice Round the Clock* (Houlston and Wright, 1859)

Schlesinger, Max, *Saunterings in and about London* (Nathaniel Cook, 1853)

I have also found the following modern works invaluable:-

Adburgham, Alison, *Shops and Shopping: 1800–1914* (Barrie & Jenkins, 1989)

Bailey, Peter (ed.), *Music Hall: The Business of Pleasure* (Open University Press, 1986)

Burnett, John, *Liquid Pleasures* (Routledge, 1999)

Bynum, W.F., *Science and the Practice of Medicine in the Nineteenth Century* (Cambridge, 1994)

Curl, James Stevens, *Kensal Green Cemetery* (Phillimore, 2001)

Dyos, H.J. & Wolff, Michael (ed.), *The Victorian City* (Routledge, 1978)

Ehrman, Edwina, et al., *London Eats Out: 1500–2000* (Philip Wilson, 2000)

Evans, Keith, *The Development of the English School System* (Hodder & Stoughton, 1985)

Girouard, Mark, *Victorian Pubs* (Studio Vista, 1975)

Halliday, Stephen, *The Great Stink of London* (Sutton, 1999)

Halliday, Stephen, *Underground to Everywhere* (Sutton, 2001)

Meller, Hugh, *London Cemeteries* (Avebury, 1981)

Nead, Lynda, *Victorian Babylon* (Yale, 2000)

Olsen, Donald J., *The Growth of Victorian London* (Penguin, 1976)

Weinreb, Ben, & Hibbert, Christopher, *The London Encyclopaedia*, (Macmillian, 1983)

Wohl, Anthony S., *Endangered Lives: Public Health in Victorian Britain* (Methuen, 1984)

CHRONOLOGY

In this book, I have taken the Victoria era to be defined by Queen Victoria's time on the throne: 1837–1901. Where I have included events immediately preceding this period or mentioned things happening shortly afterward, I hope the reader will forgive me.

The highly selective chronology below concentrates on London-related buildings and incidents mentioned in the text.

Houses of Parliament

1837 – Queen Victoria accedes to the throne; Euston railway station opens; West Norwood Cemetery opens; typhus epidemic.

1838 – Regent Street Polytechnic opens, providing popular science demonstrations; Paddington railway station opens.

1839 – Highgate Cemetery opens.

1840 – Nunhead, Abney Park and Brompton cemeteries open.

1841 – Tower Hamlets Cemetery opens; London Library opens to subscribers; Fenchurch Street railway station opens.

1842 – Bagnigge Wells Pleasure Gardens close; Detective Department of Metropolitan Police formed; Pentonville 'Model' Prison opens; Mudie's lending library opens on New Oxford Street.

1843 – Theatre Regulation Act; Thames Tunnel from Wapping to Rotherhithe completed.

1844 – Ragged School Union founded to educate the poor; Society for Improving the Condition of the Labouring Classes founded to supply 'model housing'.

1845 – Victoria Park opens; Hungerford Suspension Bridge opens.

1846 – Baths and Washhouses Act enables building of public baths and laundries.

1847 – New Oxford Street completed.

1848 – Cholera epidemic; Queen's College for training governesses opens; Waterloo railway station opens.

1850 – North London Collegiate School for Girls opens.

1851 – Great Exhibition in Hyde Park; Wyld's Great Globe opens in Leicester Square (demolished 1861).

1852 – London Diorama near Regent's Park converted into chapel; Canterbury Music Hall opens in Lambeth; King's Cross railway station opens.

1854 – Great Exhibition reopens at Sydenham (destroyed by fire in 1936); Brookwood Cemetery opens; St Pancras Cemetery in Finchley opens; John Snow maps spread of cholera in Soho.

1855 – Metropolitan Board of Works created; Victoria Dock opens.

1857 – British Museum Reading Room opens; South Kensington Museum opens; first public library in London opens in Great Smith Street, Westminster.

1858 – 'The Great Stink', the filthy River Thames emits a revolting odour; General Medical Council, for regulating doctors, established; Chelsea Bridge opens.

1859 – Vauxhall Pleasure Gardens close.

1860 – Victoria railway station opens.

1862 – International Exhibition at Kensington; William Frith's painting *The Railway Station* on view at the Royal Academy; Hugh Pilkington MP garrotted; Lambeth Bridge opens.

1863 – Football Association formed; Whiteleys department store founded in Bayswater; Metropolitan underground railway opens from Farringdon to Paddington.

1864 – First Peabody housing project opens in Spitalfields; Hungerford Suspension Bridge replaced by rail and foot bridge.

1865 – Burford's Panorama in Leicester Square closes.

1866 – Cholera epidemic in East End; Cannon Street railway station opens; Millwall Dock opens.

1867 – Crossness Pumping Station opens; Metropolitan Asylums Board created, new fever hospitals created; Pantheon Bazaar on Oxford Street closes.

1868 – Gaiety Restaurant and Theatre open on the Strand; Michael Barrett is the last person to be hanged in public; Abbey Mills Pumping Station opens; St Pancras railway station opens.

1869 – Holborn Viaduct opens.

1870 – Victoria Embankment completed; Education Act allows creation of London School Board and 'Board Schools'; Tower Subway under Thames opens (closed 1894).

1871 – Annual 'International Exhibitions' begin at Kensington; first F.A. Cup played; new St Thomas's Hospital opens by Westminster Bridge; Army and Navy Stores open near Victoria; Queen Victoria Street completed.

1873 – Alexandra Palace opens, and promptly burns down; Lawn Tennis ('Sphairistike') invented; Midland Grand Hotel opens above St Pancras Station.

1874 – Criterion Restaurant and Theatre open in Piccadilly; Northumberland Avenue completed; Liverpool Street railway station opens.

1875 – Colosseum near Regent's Park demolished; building begins on Bedford Park housing estate at Turnham Green; Liberty department store founded.

1877 – Cremorne Pleasure Gardens close; first men's tennis championship at Wimbledon; Shaftesbury Park model housing estate finished in Battersea.

1878 – London University admits women to degree subjects, except medicine; Temple Bar pulled down to ease traffic in Fleet Street; *Princess Alice* pleasure steamer disaster on River Thames.

1879 – London University permits women to obtain medical degrees.

1880 – Horsemonger Lane Gaol demolished; education made compulsory in London for five- to ten-year olds; Royal Arcade opens near Bond Street; Albert Dock opens.

1881 – Natural History Museum opens on site of International Exhibition; Regent Street Polytechnic acquired by Quintin Hogg for education of working people; Queen's Park model housing estate finished.

1882 – First defeat of England by Australia at the Oval cricket ground.

1883 – Northampton Institute founded in Clerkenwell (later City University).

1884 – Eagle Tavern and Pleasure Gardens sold to Salvation Army; first women's tennis championship at Wimbledon; linking of District and Metropolitan underground railway lines creates Circle line.

1885 – Soho Bazaar closes.

1886 – Colonial and Indian Exhibition at Kensington; Shaftesbury Avenue

Queen Victoria

completed; Blackfriars railway station opens.

1887 – American Exhibition at Earl's Court; Charing Cross Road completed; Victoria's Golden Jubilee.

1888 – 'Jack the Ripper' murders in Whitechapel.

1889 – Savoy Hotel opens; Queen Anne's Mansions ('monster' block of flats) completed; dockers' strike.

1890 – 'Scotland Yard' relocates to buildings on the Embankment.

1892 – Whitechapel Public Library opens.

1894 – Tower Bridge opens.

1895 – Great Wheel erected at Earl's Court (demolished 1907); cycling craze in Battersea Park.

1896 – First demonstrations of cinema in London; first cars seen in London.

1897 – Tate Gallery opens on site of former Millbank Prison; Victoria's Diamond Jubilee; Blackwall Tunnel under River Thames completed.

1900 – Wallace Collection opens in Manchester Square; underground railway Central line, from Liverpool Street to Shepherd's Bush, opens.

1901 – Death of Queen Victoria.

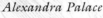

Alexandra Palace

MUSEUMS & GALLERIES

The list below provides contact details for a wide range of London museums. I have included institutions that were welcoming visitors in the nineteenth century, such as Sir John Soane's Museum, homes of eminent Victorians, such as Dickens House, and modern museums that touch on various aspects of Victorian life, such as London's Transport Museum.

If you are visiting London for the first time, the Museum of London provides the best overview of London's history, and is perhaps a good place to start.

As always, *visitors are advised to telephone or check websites for precise opening hours and prices, before they visit.* (NB: Some museums listed here as *Free* may charge for special exhibitions or large tour groups.)

The Bank of England Museum
Threadneedle Street
London EC2R 8AH
tel. 020 7601 5491
www.bankofengland.co.uk/museum
Contents: History of the Bank of England and coinage.
Free entrance

Bramah Museum of Tea and Coffee
40 Southwark Street
London SE1 1UN
tel. 020 7403 5650
www.bramahmuseum.co.uk
Contents: History of tea and coffee over the last 400 years.
Entrance charge

The British Museum
Great Russell Street
London WC1B 3DG
tel. 020 7323 8000
www.thebritishmuseum.ac.uk
Contents: Art and antiquities from ancient to modern times.
Free entrance

Brunel Engine House and Tunnel Museum
Railway Avenue, Rotherhithe
London SE16 4LF
tel. 020 8806 4325
Contents: Exhibition on the Thames Tunnel in its old engine house; ring in advance.
Entrance charge

Carlyle's House
24 Cheyne Row, Chelsea
London SW3 5HL
tel. 020 7352 7087
www.nationaltrust.org.uk/places/
carlyleshouse/index.html
Contents: House of Victorian critic Thomas Carlyle, 'The Sage of Chelsea'.
Entrance charge

Dickens House
48 Doughty Street
London WC1N 2LX
tel. 020 7405 2127
www.dickensmuseum.com
Contents: Charles Dickens's home 1837–9; includes manuscripts and items associated with Dickens.
Entrance charge

Florence Nightingale Museum
2 Lambeth Palace Road
London SE1 7EW
tel. 020 7620 0374
www.florence-nightingale.co.uk
Contents: Items associated with Florence Nightingale; history of nursing.
Entrance charge

The Geffrye Museum
Kingsland Road
London E2 8EA
tel. 020 7739 9893
www.geffrye-museum.org.uk
Contents: British domestic interiors displayed by period.
Free entrance

Horniman Museum
100 London Road, Forest Hill
London SE23 3PQ
tel. 020 8699 1872
www.horniman.ac.uk
Contents: Anthropology, natural history and musical instruments.
Free entrance

Jewish Museum
129–131 Albert Street
London NW1 7NB
tel. 020 7284 1997
www.jewishmuseum.org.uk
Contents: Jewish history and religious life.
Entrance charge

Sir John Soane's Museum
13 Lincoln's Inn Fields
London WC2A 3BP
tel. 020 7405 2107
www.soane.org
Contents: Sir John Soane's collection of art and antiquities.
Free entrance

Kew Gardens
Richmond
Surrey TW9 3AB
tel. 020 8332 5655
www.rbgkew.org.uk
Contents: Botanic gardens, including iron & glass Palm House built 1844–8.
Entrance charge

Leighton House
12 Holland Park Road
London W14 8LZ
tel. 020 7602 3316
www.rbkc.gov.uk/
leightonhousemuseum
Contents: House of Victorian artist Lord Leighton, includes paintings and exotic interior decoration, most famously the Arab Hall.
Entrance charge

Linley Sambourne House
18 Stafford Terrace
London W8 7BH
tel. 020 7602 3316
www.rbkc.gov.uk/
linleysambournehouse
Contents: House of Victorian cartoonist Linley Sambourne.
Entrance charge

London Fire Brigade Museum
London Fire & Emergency Planning Authority
8 Albert Embankment
London SE1 7SD
tel. 020 7587 2000
www.london-fire.gov.uk/about_us/
our_history/our_history.asp
Contents: History of the Fire Brigade.
Entrance charge

London's Transport Museum
Covent Garden Piazza
London WC2E 7BB
tel. 020 7565 7299
www.ltmuseum.co.uk
Contents: History of transport in
London – rail, omnibus, tram, tube
etc.
Entrance charge

MCC Museum
Lord's Cricket Ground
St John's Wood
London NW8 8QN
www.lords.org/history/museum.asp
Contents: History of cricket and
Marylebone Cricket Club.
Entrance charge

Museum in Docklands
No. 1 Warehouse, West India Quay,
Hertsmere Road
London E14 4AL
tel. 0870 444 3856
www.museumindocklands.org.uk
Contents: History of London's port
and docklands.
Entrance charge

Museum of Childhood
Cambridge Heath Road
London E2 9PA
tel. 020 8980 2415
www.vam.ac.uk/vastatic/nmc/index.
html
Contents: History of childhood;
principally toys.
Free entrance

Museum of London
London Wall
London EC2Y 5HN
tel. 0870 444 3852
www.museum-london.org.uk
Contents: History of London through
the centuries.
Free entrance

The National Gallery
Trafalgar Square
London WC2N 5DN
tel. 020 7747 2885
www.nationalgallery.org.uk
Contents: Art.
Free entrance

The Natural History Museum
Cromwell Road
London SW7 5BD
tel. 020 7942 5011
www.nhm.ac.uk
Contents: Natural history.

Free entrance

National Maritime Museum
Park Row, Greenwich
London SE10 9NF
tel. 020 8312 6565
www.nmm.ac.uk
Contents: British maritime history.
Free entrance

**The Old Operating Theatre
Museum**
9a St Thomas Street
London SE1 9RY
tel. 020 7955 4791
www.thegarret.org.uk
Contents: Authentic nineteenth-
century operating theatre; history
of medicine.
Entrance charge

Ragged School Museum
46–50 Copperfield Road
London E3 4RR
tel. 020 8980 6405
www.raggedschoolmuseum.org.uk
Contents: History of the Ragged
Schools and of the Copperfield Road
school in particular.
Free entrance

The Royal Artillery Museum
Royal Arsenal, Woolwich
London SE18 6ST
tel. 020 8855 7755
www.firepower.org.uk
Contents: History of the Woolwich
Arsenal weapons manufactory.
Entrance charge

Royal London Hospital Museum
Royal London Hospital, Whitechapel
London E1 1BB
tel. 020 7377 7608
www.brlcf.org.uk
Contents: History of the hospital from
1740 onwards.
Free entrance

The Science Museum
Exhibition Road
South Kensington
London SW7 2DD
tel. 0870 870 4868
www.sciencemuseum.org.uk
Contents: History of science and
technology.
Free entrance

The Sherlock Holmes Museum
221b Baker Street
London NW1 6XE
tel. 020 7935 8866
www.sherlock-holmes.co.uk
Contents: Recreation of Holmes's
study; memorabilia.
Entrance charge

Tate Britain
Millbank
London SW1P 4RG
tel. 020 7887 8000
www.tate.org.uk/britain/default.htm
Contents: Art.
Free entrance

Theatre Museum
Russell Street, Covent Garden
London WC2E 7PR
tel. 020 7943 4700
theatremuseum.vam.ac.uk/
Contents: History of theatre in
London.
Free entrance

Victoria and Albert Museum
Cromwell Road, South Kensington
London SW7 2RL
tel. 020 7942 2000
www.vam.ac.uk
Contents: History of art and design.
Free entrance

The Wallace Collection
Hertford House, Manchester Square
London W1U 3BN
tel. 020 7563 9500
www.wallacecollection.org
Contents: Various art treasures,
including armoury, ceramics and
paintings.
Free entrance

Wapping Hydraulic Power Station
Wapping Wall
London E1W 3ST
tel. 020 7680 2080
Contents: Restaurant and art gallery
in converted 1890 power station.
Free entrance

William Morris Gallery
Lloyd Park, Forest Road
London E17 4PP
tel. 020 8527 3782
www.lbwf.gov.uk/wmg/home.htm
Contents: Life and works of William
Morris.
Free entrance

INDEX

PICTURE ACKNOWLEDGEMENTS

All pictures supplied by Eric Nathan except for the following:
Albert Arzoz: Pages 10 & 23
©Copyright The British Museum: Page 16
Chris Coe: Pages 44 (right), 48, 55
John Crook: Page 11 (bottom)
The Dawes Collection: Page 21 (bottom)
The Geffrye Museum: Page 109
Courtesy of Friends of Herne Hill Velodrome: Page 33
Company Archive, Harrods Ltd, London: Page 124
The Illustrated London News Picture Library: Pages 26, 28, 29 (top), 32 (top), 38 (bottom), 56 (bottom), 57 (right), 71, 79, 89 (bottom), 94, 103, 106, 121, 126, 131 (top), 133, 138 (top), 150 (top), 154, 155
Sir John Soane's Museum/Martin Charles: Page 19
Courtesy of Richard Jones: Page 22
Mary Evans Picture Library: Pages 52 (top), 63, 66, 72, 76 (bottom), 78 (bottom), 91 (bottom), 93, 96, 136 (bottom), 141 (top), 146
Courtesy of Marylebone Cricket Ground: Page 32 (bottom)
Courtesy of the Molyneux family (picture taken by Eric Nathan): Page 70 (top)
The National Archives Image Library: Page 51
Courtesy of the North London Collegiate School: Page 95 (bottom)
The Raymond Mander & Joe Mitchenson Theatre Collection: Pages 24 & 29 (bottom)
Roger Vaughan Picture Library: Page 21 (top)
Courtesy of Thomas Cook AG: Page 23 (top)
John Thomson: Pages 37, 49, 90, 128 (bottom), 139 (top)
University College London Library Services: Page 60
Courtesy of the University of Exeter Library (The Bill Douglas Centre for the History of Cinema and Popular Culture): Page 20 (top)
The Wellcome Trust: Pages 75, 76 (top), 77, 80 (bottom), 85 (top)
Courtesy of Wimbledon Lawn Tennis Museum: Page 31